PRAISE FOR
TWO WOMEN, ONE WAR

"Women played an important and fascinating role in the US war in Vietnam, but little is known about them. *Two Women, One War* begins to remedy this with the true story of the fifty-year friendship between a South Vietnamese (Viet Cong) revolutionary and an American Quaker."
—**Jane Fonda,** actor and activist

"Mai's story touches all of us because it addresses missed opportunities. Had my father met Mai during his tenure as Secretary of Defense, maybe he would have realized the folly of the Vietnam War and ended it long before the loss of millions of lives."
—**Craig McNamara**, author of *Because Our Fathers Lied: A Memoir of Truth and Family, from Vietnam to Today,* owner of Sierra Orchards, and president of Center for Land-Based Learning.

"I spent a year as a soldier in Vietnam, but I was mostly confined to the base camp of a US Army infantry brigade. I did not directly witness the suffering inflicted on Vietnamese civilians. Half a century later, Ms. Griffith's book has made that suffering vivid for me, and it offers something more. This is in part the story of a friendship between Ms. Griffith, a Quaker, and a Vietnamese woman, a revolutionary who had lost her legs to an American-made Claymore mine. They met and worked together at a rehabilitation center, where, in the midst of war and with scant resources, artificial limbs were ingeniously fashioned and fitted to civilians who had also lost arms and legs, many of them children. It is a complicated story, nicely told, sometimes tense and dramatic, and yet imbued with gentleness. War forces human beings to divide themselves into enemy camps; it creates the need and compulsion to kill and destroy. For me, this book serves as a reminder that grace and courage also have force, that human kindness can survive even war."
—**Tracy Kidder**, Pulitzer Prize-winning author of *Soul of a New Machine,* author of bestselling books *House* and *Among School Children,* and award-winning author of *Mountains Beyond Mountains* and *Rough Sleepers*

"Jane Griffith has an extraordinary story to tell about Vietnam and a woman named Mai. Jane worked as a director of the American Friends Service in Quang Ngai province, whose job it was to put prosthetic limbs on Vietnamese civilians. Mai was a Vietnamese patient, a double amputee, who developed a deep friendship with Jane. They belonged to the opposite sides of the war, but when in danger, they helped each other, and after the war, they visited each other's families. This is an unusual, compelling war story."

—**Frances FitzGerald**, author of *Fire in the Lake*, which won a Pulitzer Prize, Brancroft, and National Book Award

"This remarkable book, *Two Women, One War*, is a memoir of a fifty-year friendship between an American and Vietnamese coworker, based at a Quaker rehab center in the middle of Quang Ngai province. In this embattled place, the two worked together, assisting Vietnamese civilians who had lost their limbs. This is an intensely personal story, which provides an extraordinary vantage point for understanding the war. It moves away from matters of high policy and enables the reader to see the war from the ground up. You can almost walk down the streets of Quang Ngai City, visualize women prisoners, chained to their hospital beds, and hear the sounds of American bombs dropping in the night. And, with all that suffering and drama, learn what follows. An extraordinary achievement."

—**Carolyn Eisenberg,** author of *Fire and Rain: Nixon, Kissinger and the Wars in Southeast Asia*, the 2024 Bancroft Prize-winning 2024 history book. Professor of US History and American Foreign Policy, Hofstra University

"During the Vietnam war, Americans and Vietnamese were not only present as soldiers but also in other human roles, and people rarely read about them. Jane Barton Griffith's book is one of the few books written about these people. Jane tells the story of herself and a Vietnamese woman, who were enemies, different in education, beliefs, and family background, but who stood side by side in the most difficult circumstances and created a lifelong friendship. More specifically, Jane and my sister, Dang Thuy Tram, a female doctor who was killed in 1970, had some coincidences: They were the same age, lived in the same area, during the same period of the war, and did the same job—rescuing the wounded. If my sister were still alive, they would have many memories to share with each other. To me, this book is as authentic and engaging as Larry Berman's *Perfect Spy*. Jane writes with deep feeling about my sister. The contribution of women during the American war has been overlooked and neglected, but Jane's memoir helps remind us of the contribution of women, like my sister and Jane's best friend, Mai."

> —**Kim-Tram Dang,** sister of Dang Thuy Tram, author of internationally bestselling war diary, *Last Night I Dreamed of Peace: The Diary of Dang Thuy Tram*.

"*Two Women, One War* stands out for the courage and commitment of its two principals. It portrays, with plain-spoken clarity and candor, the scars and, yes, blessings that come with performing invaluable, painstaking, sometimes harrowing humanitarian work during the Vietnam War, in the embattled capital of South Vietnam's most war-torn province."

> —**Jaques Leslie,** war correspondent for *LA Times* and author of *The Mark: A War Correspondent's Memoir of Vietnam and Cambodia*

"Jane has a story worth telling. All war is about people. Sadly, we often learn this in the midst of events we do not understand, let alone control. We see the impact war has on people. That's what Jane learned and that's what people need to read."

> —**Bob Chenoweth**, former POW in Vietnam for five years, antiwar activist, and former curator and cultural resource manager for Nez Perce National Historical Park

"These two audacious women had the courage to face the horrors of their war, and then to face each other others' pain. In their friendship comes a profound education on a deeply traumatic conflict in recent history. I hope anyone interested in the Vietnam War, or war in general, takes a moment to read this; now, more than ever, our world aches for stories like Mai and Jane's that remind us of our shared humanity."

> —**Bo Kravis**, film producer of documentary *Wartime Civilians in Vietnam* to be aired on Netflix in April 2025

Two Women, One War:
An Unlikely Friendship During the Vietnam War
by Jane Barton Griffith

© Copyright 2025 Jane Barton Griffith

979-8-88824-613-9

All rights reserved. No part of this publication may be reproduced, stored in a retrieval system, or transmitted in any form or by any means—electronic, mechanical, photocopy, recording, or any other—except for brief quotations in printed reviews, without the prior written permission of the author.

Published by

3705 Shore Drive
Virginia Beach, VA 23455
800-435-4811
www.koehlerbooks.com

TWO WOMEN, ONE WAR

*An Unlikely Friendship
During the Vietnam War*

Jane Barton Griffith
with voice of Nguyễn thi Mai

VIRGINIA BEACH
CAPE CHARLES

INTRODUCTION

I NEVER INTENDED to go to Vietnam.

Yet it was the beginning of the greatest adventure of my life and the opportunity to develop a deep friendship with a Vietnamese woman, Mai. Our story is a universal tale of friendship between two women during a war, women of different races, languages, physical abilities, religious backgrounds, and educational levels, who overcame barriers to become sisters. We grew to love and understand each other despite our countries wanting us to be enemies. Our friendship has lasted more than fifty years, a connection sustained through letters, emails, and visits. In 2017, during a visit, Mai placed a letter in my lap with a firm command—"Read this!"—and pointed to the beginning of the letter I had written fourteen years earlier.

> Dearest Sister Mai,
>   . . . *We really should write a book together. . . . Our story is not about us. It is a metaphor of the true story of the Vietnamese people and the American war years and the power of friendship and love across all barriers.*
>
>   *One reason I feel strongly about this is that the war is described in our history books from the point of view of America. Nearly three million men served in Vietnam, and they each had a story. Our libraries are full of their memoirs.*[1] *We need to write our story so young people, in the future, will hear our voices too.*

When I looked up from reading, Mai said, "It's time to write that book, Jane."

---

1 Nearly 30,000 of them.

CHAPTER 1

Going to Vietnam

I thought I was ready for the challenge of working in a war zone. My first experience in Vietnam—a flight on a domestic airline—dispelled that.

When my then husband, David, and I arrived in Saigon, we were hit with a blast of tropical heat. Helicopters buzzed overhead and landed around us. Heat waves in rainbow colors rose from the tarmac. I inhaled foreign scents. The humidity was oppressive. We puzzled over which line to stand in to have our visas stamped, a task undertaken in a manner inherited from the French—not just once but multiple times, with loud, affirmative thumps.

Moving past customs, we searched for the departure gate to Quảng Ngãi. Hard plastic seats in the waiting area were filled with families—three or four people leaning against each other, eyes closed and mouths open, women nursing babies. Everyone carried bags and packages of multiple sizes; some were wrapped with tape, others bulged with fruit, and some tall packages resembled mummies.

There was no formal queuing, nor were tickets collected. Instead, when our departure gate opened, people surged forward as if a plug had been released. Though there were seats for everyone, the market women seemed to panic at the stress of securing a place on the plane. They were bringing produce from the south to sell in Quảng Ngãi where the war had devastated most fruit trees. Not getting on that plane meant they would lose their financial investment. Amid this chaos, we boarded the small civilian plane that would transport us to an unfamiliar world for the next three years.

We flew over jungles of vivid greens pockmarked with raw wounds from bombs. I began to learn about the scarring of the land. Artillery fire made small pockmarks. Delayed fuse bombs left holes as big as swimming pools. Antipersonnel bombs drew a pattern in the ground—yellow asterisks emanating rays. The earth was black where napalm had been dropped, and lush mountain foliage lay scattered, as if scratched with a gargantuan rake. The impact of bombs had blown off the tops of trees, leaving swaths of decapitated trunks. Our destination, the provincial capital of Quảng Ngãi, had the greatest civilian damage of any place in Vietnam. As our plane descended, vomit slid from the floor behind me and wet my shoes. I later learned that many Vietnamese, unaccustomed to air travel in those days, became airsick.

Quảng Ngãi City

The heat was crushing. Sweat streamed between my breasts. A white Volkswagen bus spotted with rust was waiting for us. We were urged to get in quickly because the arrival of late afternoon planes triggered mortaring of the airport. The US military and the Army of the Republic of Vietnam (ARVN) maintained small circles of control in and around Quảng Ngãi, but the rest of the province belonged to the enemy, mostly guerilla fighting forces calling themselves the National Liberation Front (NLF), a revolutionary movement to overthrow the South Vietnamese government and unite Vietnam. The US called them the Viet Cong.

I felt as if I had arrived on a Western movie set. The town consisted of one-story buildings; the roads were dirt. Mangy dogs and chickens roamed the streets. I saw what I assumed to be a "bus"—a horse-drawn wooden flatbed with benches filled with passengers on each side, a canvas top protecting them from the roasting sun. A taxi, with three wheels, looked like a toy.

Along the roadside, women walked with lilting steps, each carrying a flexible bamboo pole over one shoulder, heavy baskets attached to both ends. The women's gait appeared to suspend them in the air for a split second. There were few motorized vehicles, mostly scooters and motorcycles, sometimes carrying an entire family or ten or more pigs in stacked crates. It was then I had my first encounter with a US military vehicle: a five-ton truck with a screeching, high-pitched air horn. Its immense frame, on giant wheels, dominated the narrow street. They might not have been as loud as antipersonnel carriers with metal treads, but their horns were terrifying. Mounted on the outside of the truck, they could reach earsplitting decibels. Drivers leaned on the horns to scare everything off the road, but an occasional human or animal was run down. I still have nightmares of those thundering trucks and wake with a jerk as my body tries to jump out of the way.

Orienting

David and I began our work as codirectors of the humanitarian projects run by the AFSC. The main focus of Quaker humanitarian work in Vietnam was the AFSC Rehabilitation Center located in a hotbed of Viet Cong activity. The US military nicknamed the area "Pinkville" because the population was controlled by "red Communists." The Center was five miles from My Lai, where US soldiers had slaughtered more than five hundred Vietnamese civilians. My new job overlapped with the outgoing director, Lou Kubica, an experience that is mostly a blur. Lou—who later became a Buddhist priest and rarely spoke of the war—was anxious to leave. I remember him saying, "The Vietnamese are a deeply wise, subtle, and remarkable people with a long-term view of history. You will never have an experience as important as this one."

I dismissed his remark. My life was already filled with fascinating experiences. Three years in Vietnam weren't going to be my life's pinnacle. Perhaps this Midwestern director and his English wife had led a sheltered existence. I, however, had traveled internationally, benefited from a remarkable family with educator parents, and attended an expensive private college. As it turned out, his words were prescient. Vietnam shook my foundations and understanding of the world. It was life-altering.

AFSC House and Setting

The AFSC house was on Phan Bội Châu Street, named for a nineteenth-century scholar who, after passing the highest level of Mandarin exams, organized his own social class to drive the French out of Vietnam. If the American military had studied Vietnamese history, they would have learned of the 3,000-year struggle of the Vietnamese to end domination by the Chinese, Japanese, and French. It was ironic that a major street in the provincial capital, named for a famous nationalist who opposed foreign domination, was now occupied by a foreign power, the US.

My new home was a stucco building the same color as the dirt in the courtyard. Its windows had shutters but no glass or screens. At the back of the house, an attached room with thick concrete walls served as a bunker. The kitchen was an open space, partly roofed with sheets of corrugated metal, where a Vietnamese woman sat peeling and preparing vegetables—her artificial leg hampering her from accomplishing the traditional Vietnamese squat.

Like the Vietnamese, our meals consisted of mostly vegetables. Rice was put into small bowls, and we reached with chopsticks toward the Center of the table to select a few vegetables and, occasionally, some meat or fish. We sprinkled roasted chopped peanuts and fermented fish sauce on top. The Vietnamese loved to tell us of the days before the war, when pigs, chickens, and fish were plentiful. Bananas grew in twenty varieties, and everyone had their own supply. Each house had a small vegetable garden, bougainvillea vines stretching over the doorways, and flowers growing in ceramic containers.

After a few months in Vietnam, I mentioned to an American soldier that we ate the same food as the Vietnamese people. He exclaimed, "My god, you eat on the economy." At first, I didn't know what he meant, but I came to understand that "on the economy" referred to food grown in Vietnam, not flown in from the US.

US soldiers lived on bases where American life was recreated—with bars, bowling alleys, movie theaters, and shops selling US goods at reduced rates—resulting in a bizarre juxtaposition of life within a military compound and the life of the Vietnamese people surrounding it. Once, on a visit to the nearest military base, I witnessed incoming helicopters, carrying seriously wounded and dead soldiers, landing near an outdoor movie theater where other soldiers relaxed and drank American beer.

A curfew restricted us to the AFSC house at night where we often sat in our "family room," socializing among ourselves and listening to stories from our teammates who came from different geographic and economic backgrounds. The doctor's family raised pigs that ate waste chocolate from a candy manufacturing factory. The physical therapist's family in the US south was shunned because they supported integration. One young man was an Asian scholar who had studied Chinese language in Taiwan.

This was also where we met with journalists who came to stay because there were no hotels in Quảng Ngãi. Access to the AFSC team was a resource for journalists, as we were known for being an excellent source of war and regional information. The AFSC house abutted Vietnamese houses on all sides, with shared fences, and when we traveled to the countryside, we spoke with the Vietnamese people and listened to their accounts of the war. We observed the war's effects firsthand. By contrast, the US military, ARVN, and the Central Intelligence Agency (CIA) isolated themselves from the population in separate fortified compounds with sandbags and barbed wire. Only a few American military had any Vietnamese language training, so their sources of information were English-speaking Vietnamese people indebted to them for salaries and positions. They told the Americans what they wanted to hear.

At the AFSC house, a closet had been converted into a darkroom by a former team member, who had traveled to Hong Kong to buy the necessary equipment and chemicals to develop film negatives. I had bought a camera, a 35-millimeter with changeable lenses. The war was in front of me, and I just pointed my camera and clicked. In a way, the camera put a layer between me and the rawness of the war. One day a Jeep-load of bodies and body parts pulled into the grounds of our Rehabilitation Center. As I took photographs, a boy climbed down from the back of the vehicle, holding his little sister in his arms. He pleaded, "Help, help me." I thought her head was bent backward—until I realized her head was missing.

The horrors of war seemed less personal through a lens. I recognized I was using the camera to shield myself, yet there were also frequent occasions when I refrained from shooting photos. I was not an observing foreigner, like a journalist, but someone working side-by-side with the Vietnamese. I did not want to intrude into their privacy.

Boys at Rehabilitation Center school for patients and siblings

Not all my photos were tragic. I processed many of shy, giggling children, their arms around each other's shoulders, like kids far from a war zone. In our darkroom, dimpled faces peeking from under traditional cone-shaped hats or an elderly gentleman, in his black ao dai proudly walking in a rice field at the Lunar New Year emerged from the shadows of the chemicals in the enamel trays.

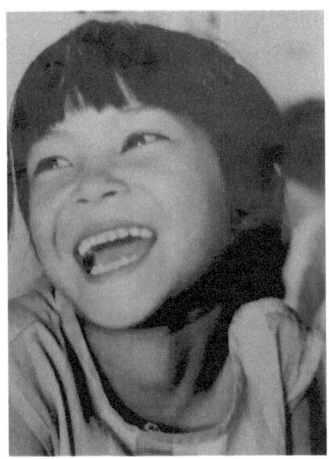

Siblings of patients at Rehabilitation Center school

Below-knee amputee who received the loan of a treadle sewing machine

The bedroom David and I shared and a guest room were on the second floor of the house. Some nights I'd read on a wood sofa, although a single light bulb could produce so much heat that I sometimes turned it off and sat in the dark. As in most of the rooms, a fan rotated when we had intermittent power. I don't remember a cool breeze, only the heat, the insufferable heat of summer months and the humidity of the monsoon season that caused green mold to grow on my leather shoes.

It was traditional for the Western and Vietnamese staff to rest after lunch. I'd wake from these naps in a pool of sweat, my brain fogged and my body in slow motion, as if an ether-soaked handkerchief was dragging me to another dimension. I became afraid of falling asleep, and it became my custom to read during the rest period. It was one way I kept control over my life in a war zone, by staying alert and awake. I read up on my interests at the time, Japanese textiles and ceramics from ancient kiln sites, topics of beauty and timelessness.

Incoming or Outgoing?

I'm not sure if visitors were able to sleep. Journalist Jacques Leslie wrote, "I thought the two Quakers, Jane and David . . . were courageous simply for living in a place where rifle exchanges were regular nighttime occurrences."[2] But I disagreed. It was normal in Quảng Ngãi. We had become proficient at sensing, instantly, the source of a loud sound. We were experts in determining the distinct whine of shells and able to identify if they were "incoming" toward our house or aimed at other targets, like the electric plant. We recognized the thunderous boom of "outgoing" 105-millimeter cannons, which blasted shells toward the enemy NLF somewhere in the jungle and mountains.

Visitors would startle at the sounds. As soon as one of us called "outgoing," everyone relaxed. If incoming screeches rose in volume, it meant the rockets or artillery were getting closer. That's when we discussed heading to the bunker. If US planes were attacking an enemy outpost far from the city, we might even climb upstairs onto the flat

---

2 Leslie, Jacques, *The Mark*, Four Walls Eight Windows, New York/London, 1995, p. 165.

roof to watch the bright flashes of color. "Puff, the Magic Dragon" in action was one of the most spectacular displays. These AC-47 gunships were fitted with mini guns that "puffed" 6,000 rounds a minute. The bursts of color reminded me of sparklers we swirled in the air for the Fourth of July, except this light show was bigger and more deadly.

At night, alone in their beds, our guests had to make their own inferences about the noises. Once, the sound of a rat scurrying under the bed, combined with the sounds of rapid fire from a helicopter, woke a guest sleeping in the room next to me. When I heard moaning through the thin wall, I wondered whether to knock on his door to offer comfort. *Will it embarrass him? Should I wait for him to ask for help?* I fell back asleep. He left the next day.

Sign at entrance to Quaker Rehabilitation Center

The focus of AFSC humanitarian programs was to train Vietnamese as prosthetists and physical therapists to provide artificial arms and legs to war-injured civilians on all sides of the conflict. Of twenty trainees, several were former patients who had lost legs.

This effort took place at the Rehabilitation Center made of modest concrete blocks and sheets of metal weighted down with sandbags on the roof. At the door hung a sign: "No weapons are allowed in this building. Each patient has been injured by war machinery."

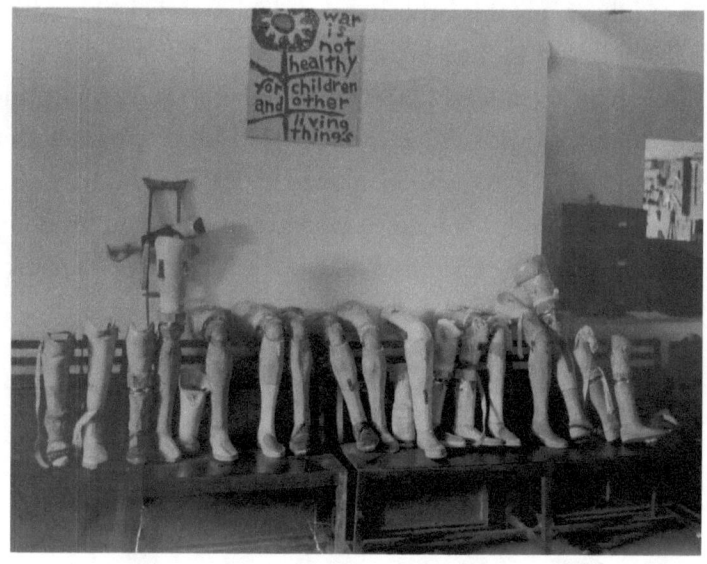

Patient's prosthetic limbs placed on bench at the end of the work day below an anti-war poster on wall issued by Another Mother for Peace

When I entered the Center each day, I saw as many as a hundred badly injured patients, all of them missing limbs. Although the Center treated mostly amputees, therapists also provided physical therapy to burn patients to keep their muscles flexible. One of the AFSC doctors described the burn ward at the hospital next door.

It is dressing-changing time for the ten to fifteen patients, mostly children, in the burn ward building at the Quảng Ngãi Hospital in Vietnam. A mother or other family member will often try to ease the bandages off as gently as possible, softening the adherent areas with soapy water. The burn victim will grit her teeth from the pain. The pus- and blood-stained bandages are dropped in a pile on the floor. The child waits 'til a nurse comes and cleans the burned area with soap and water, applying an antiseptic ointment and bandages. The child is stoic, but tears are silent markers on her cheeks.

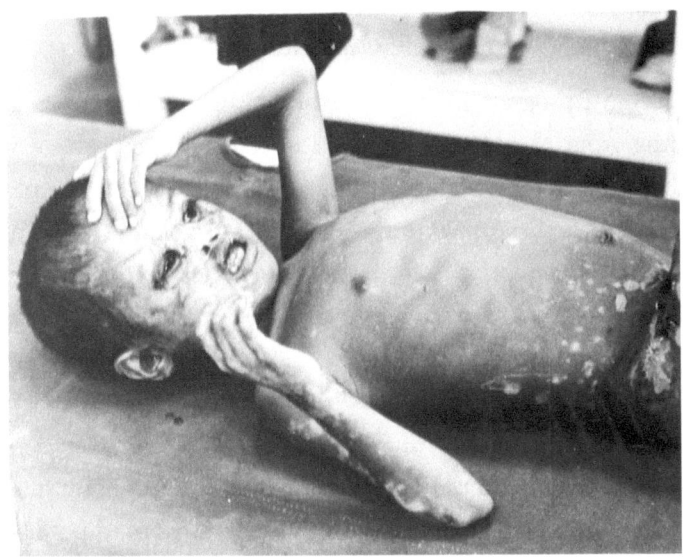

Child burned and blinded by napalm burns

Children with burns on both front and back of the body are especially unfortunate because the mattresses on the sheetless beds are covered with a piece of rubberized cloth that sticks to their bandages. And flies crawl all over the body unless constantly fanned off by a family member. Also, more unfortunate than some others are those whose faces are burned because, among other problems, scars may form, which pull the eyelids open, making it impossible to blink or close the eyes.

Treatment at the Quảng Ngãi Hospital can seem . . . medieval. There is no pain medication stronger than aspirin to relieve the severe pain and shock that is always present for the first day or two of a bad burn. And there are no blood counts or chemistries available to help assess and correct the patient's condition, which is often critical. No bacterial tests can be done to find out what type of infection is present. . . . There isn't even a thermometer on the whole burn ward, and no records are kept on the patients.[3]

AFSC Mission

The AFSC program included medical visits to prisoners, an action stemming from the Quaker conviction that all people have value, "light" within. With a history of being imprisoned for some of their own beliefs, Quakers have traditionally taken an interest in prison reform and opposed prisons as a response to societal problems. During the war, AFSC was the only Western nongovernmental organization working inside prisons in Vietnam.

Many voluntary organizations were trying to do good in Vietnam. There were organizations with religious affiliations and even a "Peace Corps," the International Voluntary Service, funded by the US government. The war generated thousands of refugees and populations in need of food and shelter. It was an endless effort. Sometimes agencies seemed to be doing the "mop-up" work of the military.

AFSC didn't peddle religion, and not all staff were Quaker. AFSC refused any US government funds. The dramatic difference between AFSC programs and those of other nongovernmental humanitarian organizations was that we were training Vietnamese in vital skills needed in a time of war. We planned to replace ourselves with certified Vietnamese staff. The AFSC Rehabilitation Center was the only location in South Vietnam where a civilian could receive a leg or arm or wheelchair at no cost, regardless of his or her political affiliation.

Since our true and larger goal was to end US involvement in the war, the most important work had to be done in the United States. Unless we addressed the root of the problem, the war itself, AFSC was just another humanitarian arm of the US military war effort. AFSC believed by living and working with the Vietnamese people, while witnessing the

---

3   Ferger, John, AFSC Report, January 23, 1972.

war firsthand, we brought credibility to our antiwar work in the US. By writing and speaking about the horrendous impact of war on civilians, we hoped Americans would see the Vietnamese as people with dignity and aspirations who wanted independence for their country—not as anonymous people often vilified with racist terms like "gooks."

Dangerous Territory

Few Americans, except those who served in the military, recognize the city or province where I worked. If I tell them Quảng Ngãi was the place described in Tim O'Brien's book, *The Things They Carried*, they might nod. In his book, *The Military Half,* Jonathan Schell gives a frontline view of the devastation in Quảng Ngãi in 1968 as he accompanies pilots on bombing raids through the province.[4] While Quảng Ngãi is renowned for the My Lai massacres, less mentioned are brutal civilian murders by South Korean Blue Dragon troops, in nearby Binh Hoa.[5]

Occasionally, when I talk about my time in Vietnam, someone's eyebrows will shoot up as they utter, "My god, you weren't in Vietnam. You were in Quảng Ngãi. Shit." The province had a revolutionary history and had been under the authority of the Viet Minh and NLF, which is why US, Korean, and ARVN troops were never able to control it.

During the entire time I worked in Quảng Ngãi Province, only the capital city and American military base at the edge of town were under the authority of the US and South Vietnamese governments. Route 1, the narrow two-lane road stretching from North to South Vietnam, was often closed because military action made it unsafe to travel. It was common to be told by villagers, with a chuckle, "It's about time for you to leave. Another government is coming to town shortly." I remember this happened frequently in Duc Pho and Mo

---

4   In an interview with Jenna Bush on The Today Show on September 24, 1920, Jane Fonda described Schell's book, *The Village of Ben Suc*, as the impetus for her move from France to the US to become an activist in the antiwar movement.

5   John Summers, "The Biggest Vietnam War Story That Americans Don't Talk About," Boston Globe, August 11, 2023. "Since 1999 scholars have documented 80 massacres by South Korean soldiers in three provinces totaling 9,000 civilians."

Duc, two places I visited almost weekly, depending on whether the road was passable. Many of our patients came from that area. I'd usually plan to head back to Quảng Ngãi city around 3 p.m.

The Americans dropped thousands of psychological warfare leaflets in Quảng Ngãi Province, and I sometimes picked them up to find out what the US was telling the people. If they suspected a village of harboring or supporting VC, the US would drop leaflets first, instructing people to leave because the area was now a "free fire zone," meaning anything that moved—human or animal—could be shot. But if the US received any hostile fire from a village, the military bombed without notification. Although there was constant danger of bombing, many Vietnamese chose to remain near food sources and ancestral graves rather than enter crowded refugee camps with inadequate food supplies, not to mention the humiliation of being fed and caged by foreigners. A "psy-ops" leaflet I kept for many years says, "*The Viet Cong hide among innocent women and children. If the Viet Cong in this area use you or your village for this purpose, you can expect death from the sky. So do not let the Viet Cong be the reason for the death of your loved ones.*"

The phrase "death from the sky" was unforgettable. Oh, and the message was in English, not the language of the people.

Communications

We did not have internet in Quảng Ngãi. Phone calls could be made at the post office, but international calls weren't possible. Later, when AFSC was supposed to evacuate, I went to Saigon to call headquarters. Occasionally, a telegram was sent or received at the local post office. AFSC established a numbering system to track letters from Quảng Ngãi to headquarters in Philadelphia. When a number in the chain was missing, it was clear a letter had gone astray. Letters were factual accounts of program progress or problems and observations about the war. I eagerly took on the job of writing field reports on a small manual typewriter, making carbon copies on "onion skin" paper. Today's advanced technology makes those reports seem like something from the far past.

With perspiration sometimes dripping into my typewriter, I often thought of my father, who wrote letters on a similar one in the 1930s. He was a teacher at Aleppo College in Aleppo, Syria. Since his letters traveled—unreliably—by camel, train, and ocean liner, he made copies, using flimsy blue carbon paper like I did. I wondered if his highly unusual decision to live and work in the Middle East for three years had sparked my desire for adventure. My father (and mother) opposed my going to Vietnam, yet I felt drawn to somewhere totally different from my Western cultural heritage, an "exotic" place, a war zone. I wondered if my father had experienced some of the same emotions and challenges of living in a foreign culture and speaking a new language.[6]

My father, W. Griffith Couser, in Luxor, Egypt

---

6   When I was growing up in the Boston area, my family was frequently invited to the homes of my father's former students who had immigrated to the US. One of my father's favorite students at Aleppo College was Dr. Paul Hasserjian, or "Dr. Paul" as I called him, whom my father sponsored to become an American citizen. Later, Dr. Paul brought his mother to the US, and my family visited her when I was ten years old. My father instructed me to sit at the feet of this frightening old woman dressed in black. As she spoke, Dr. Paul and my father translated, from Armenian to English, her story of the genocide of Armenians by Turks and her arduous journey across the desert to safety in Syria. I don't remember ever seeing her again, but her words and experience deeply impressed me.

Writing reports to the home office from a far-flung foreign town with dirt streets, I tasted the grit in my mouth and listened to shrieking air horns. I was starting a new phase of my life. Sitting in the small office, I reflected on the past couple of years. Previously, David and I represented a handsome, ideal couple—young, smart, good-looking, and athletic. We had a two-year honeymoon phase. Then my husband, who had just finished graduate school in international affairs, had an affair. David was fluent in languages and had passed the grueling State Department's tests to qualify as a simultaneous translator, from English to French. David accepted an assignment to accompany the president of Dahomey on a trip to the United States. After he finished, David went back to Chicago to have an affair with a woman he met along the way. In those days, 1969, there were no cell phones or email. When David didn't return on the scheduled date, I was worried—and then frantic. I was about to call the State Department and declare him missing when he walked into our apartment. Maybe I should have divorced him then, but I came from a family of old-fashioned values of loyalty. I gave David another chance, and he agreed that we should try to start over. We decided to try for a fresh start outside the country.

We searched for international positions, with a focus on Africa. With strong Quaker influences in my upbringing, I suggested we apply to the American Friends (Quaker) Service Committee (AFSC) that had openings in its Africa diplomatic program. At the time, AFSC put job candidates through two days of interviews. During the final interview, out of the blue, the director of international programs asked, "Would you two be interested in our director openings for Vietnam humanitarian programs?"

Although we had been heavily involved in antiwar activities, we had no desire to go to Vietnam. David and I believed humanitarian organizations there were collaborating with the military by fixing problems they created, like feeding thousands of refugees. The director added, "You are the kind of people we need in Vietnam. We don't want do-gooders with personal agendas. We want impartial individuals who will run our programs with eyes open, witness the war, and return to the US to change policies creating this war."

We were intrigued. A few weeks later, David and I returned to Philadelphia for more interviews. We arrived on a gray, rainy day, and I cried as I looked out the hotel window. I hadn't recovered from his infidelity.

We were offered—and accepted—the jobs and set off to visit our families. My parents were upset. I was "endangering my life and throwing away a great job in my field of study, my work at the National Gallery of Art." David's parents, especially his left-leaning father, endorsed our decision. Most of my friends wondered why I would risk going to a war zone.

We applied for visas and made appointments for vaccines and injections, including one for bubonic plague. I had no idea the same black plague that had killed nearly a third of all Europeans during the Middle Ages was still an active disease in Vietnam. During the AFSC orientation, I remember the director of the Vietnam program asking, "What do you think you will do during a rocket attack?" He described how some staff members climb to the roof of the AFSC house to "watch the fireworks" while others hide in the bunker. I couldn't imagine what it would be like. It was beyond my reality, but now the faraway war was my daily new world. The betrayal of my husband had left me with an emptiness. I recognized I needed to start counting on myself. I had left my sheltered life and was coming of age.

CHAPTER 2

Woman with No Legs

Every day I walked a quarter of a mile along the road, amid the chaos and dust, to the AFSC Rehabilitation Center. The war had forced rural people into the safer shelter of the city, and I passed houses built of bamboo and coconut leaves. There were no sidewalks. Life spilled into the street—chickens, dogs, scooters. Children urinated through open bottoms in their outfits. Women sold goods from baskets on bamboo poles, and men carried enormous loads on their bicycles, even beds. There was a dizzying swirl of colors, sounds, people, animals, and vehicles as I made my way down the street. It kept my brain on high alert.

The trick was to walk straight and confidently. People moved around me as long as they could anticipate my direction. I used this technique when I visited Vietnam years later. Every intersection was a complicated dance of motorbikes, a sophisticated weaving of riders coming from opposite directions. I followed my Quảng Ngãi method and headed straight into the disarray. As I walked, I held my breath against the stench that emanated from piles of refuse.

The Rehabilitation Center was located among other buildings at Quảng Ngãi Province Hospital. ARVN soldiers stood at the hospital gates. Despite their machine guns, they didn't seem menacing. Their jobs were tedious, and the heat made standing in the sun arduous. The Center was independent of any government and funded by private donations. South Vietnam's government hospital, on the other hand, was dysfunctional and struggled to meet patients' needs. The patient's first hurdle was transportation. Roads around Quảng Ngãi were often impassable because of fighting or lack of security. A patient might be forced to wait days or weeks until fighting stopped. Obviously, such delays in medical attention caused deaths.

Vietnamese families are like people everywhere. When a family member is injured, they are deeply distressed. Family ties are strong, and no sacrifice is too big to help their loved ones. The hospital had only three full-time Vietnamese doctors to care for the deluge of patients and manage the nursing staff.

All hospital personnel were government employees, which meant it was almost impossible to fire them. The worst that could be done was to transfer an incompetent employee to a less desirable hospital, but Quảng Ngãi was already at the bottom of the list. Nurses' salaries were so low, it wasn't unusual for them to have a second job, and they often slept through their duties. Corruption within the South Vietnamese government was omnipresent from the top levels of government down. It was common for medical staff to emulate their superiors and sell stolen medical supplies on the side.[7]

Chuck Henkel and Bich

AFSC was fortunate to have an orthopedic surgeon, Chuck Henkel, and his wife, Beverly, a nurse, on the team in 1970. Chuck recognized the wisdom and energy of one of our Vietnamese staff, Bich, whom he trained to perform excellent skin grafts. Bich and Chuck worked out of a closet converted into a small operating facility. They used local anesthesia to mitigate pain. They also lacked sterile medical gear and surgical caps. Chuck figured out how to create a cap by gathering the foot of a sock into a little top-knot and then stretching it over his head. An amusing sight to any outsider, another ingenious adaptation to life in a war zone.

One patient, Mai, was a double amputee whose legs had been

---

7   Sunday, January 27, 1972, John Ferger, Report to AFSC, p. 1-3.

amputated in a routine manner by physicians at an American military base. To prepare Mai for artificial limbs, she needed more padding of the skin to prevent her leg bone from eventually penetrating the skin. Chuck and Bich operated on Mai several times to create proper stumps. There was a three-month gap between the healing of Mai's stumps and her readiness for physical therapy and artificial legs.

I didn't meet Mai during the first months she was at the Quaker Center because she was recovering from stump surgery at the AFSC hostel, a cement building behind the main Rehab Center. The hostel was a large room with iron-frame beds in a row. Patients depended on family members from their distant communities to accompany them, so sometimes there were two or three people under or on one of the sheetless beds. The floor and walls were stained with blood, urine, and food droppings, and the patients who were able kept the room clean by sweeping with a broom made of native grasses. The hostel gave patients a place to rest and sleep while undergoing physical therapy, fittings, and gait training for prosthetic legs or arms.

It was Bich who recounted what Mai had told him about her arrival in Quảng Ngãi and her early encounters with AFSC.

> I was taken by helicopter from the Marine Military Hospital in Chu Lai to the Quảng Ngãi Hospital, landing at an open space behind the hospital. I was still wearing a cloth hospital gown with dried blood patches where it stuck to my skin. I was carried on a stretcher to the post-surgery room for two months, and then I was moved to Shelter C. There was no nursing staff at the hospital, and every patient needed a family member or friend to feed and help her. It is embarrassing to say this, but I couldn't go to the bathroom on my own. Plus I'd had many antibiotics to stop infections and was constipated. Someone gave me a small blanket, covered in dog hairs, with which I could cover myself while I went to the bathroom in a pot. Then I had the mortification of

persuading someone to empty it. I was once a whole woman who helped others. Then I had to depend on strangers to empty my smelly body waste.

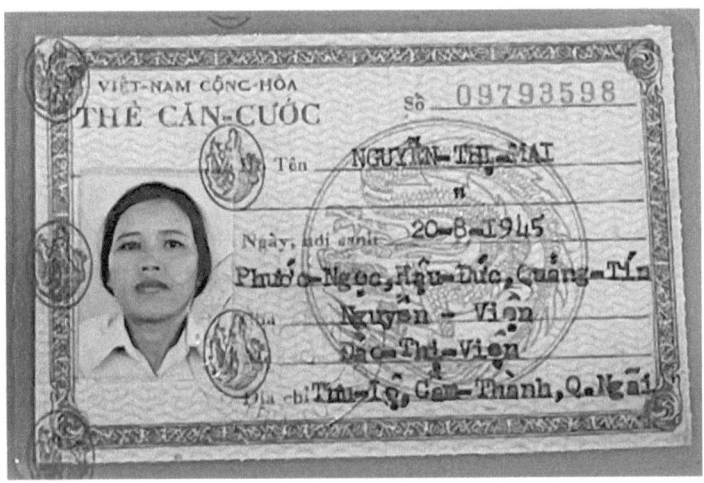

Counterfeit identity card with false name Nguyen thi Mai

After two months in Shelter C, two women came looking for potential patients—a Vietnamese, Nguyet, and an American, Caroline Elliot ["Oanh"]. This is how I came to learn about the Quaker Rehab Center. People told me that the Quaker staff fitted limbless patients with fake legs. I was curious about the project and eager to know if I might be a candidate. Once I was at the Rehab Center, I discovered that Caroline was the head of the physical therapy department, and Nguyet was a top student. After they saw me in the blood-stained gown, they brought me clothes immediately—very funny clothes—a purple blouse and hippy pants with long legs and wide bottoms in a mustard color. I would never wear loud, bright colors like that, but I was happy to have them. When Caroline told me I would be able to move into the hostel of the Rehab Center, I had hope for the first time in a year.

Bich checked on Mai's condition daily and became a close friend. Bich had a revolutionary background, having served with the Viet Minh, the Vietnamese forces that defeated the French in 1954. He had a funny, giggly laugh. When I first arrived at the Center, unable to speak a word of Vietnamese, he was my interpreter because we both spoke French.

I met Mai after her stumps had healed and she was beginning physical therapy in the Rehab Center. Weights were tin cans—with labels, like Campbell's Tomato Soup—discarded by the military base in town and filled with concrete by AFSC staff. Therapy beds were platforms made from recycled wood. Before staff arrived, Mai practiced putting her legs in and out of the prostheses. She wasn't supposed to attempt walking with any other physical therapy equipment without a staff person (or a spotter) nearby. Mai patiently waited and then practiced at the parallel bars until she was exhausted. Sometimes the physical therapist, Caroline, took Mai outside to walk on the concrete pathway outside the Center. Mai said it was strange to be up so high in the air, as if she were looking down from the treetops. She jokingly remarked that Caroline was relentless with her expectations.

> Caroline was a tough task master, and she insisted I learn how to climb stairs. There was a wooden set of stairs—with a handrail—and Caroline commanded that I repeatedly climb these stairs. I tried to persuade Caroline that Vietnamese like me live a lifestyle where I hardly ever use stairs. I told Caroline that our houses are on one level. Only fancy government buildings and homes have stairs. But Caroline wasn't dissuaded. "Climbing stairs will come in handy. You'll want to walk upstairs sometime in your life."

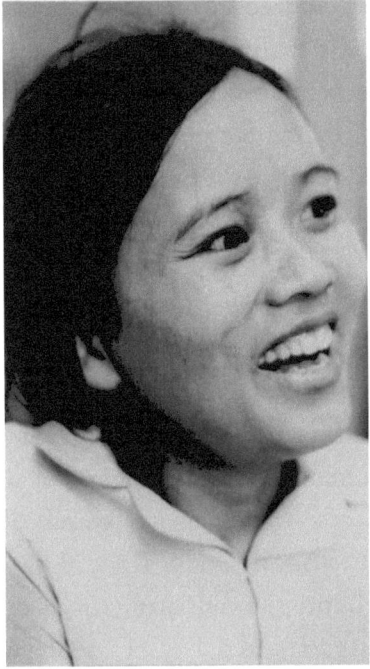

Photo of Mai

Mai Becomes an AFSC Employee

Mai was bright. She had a lively and open face that made people interested in talking to her. She was a problem solver. Soon staff suggested Mai might make a good hire for the Center. We needed a receptionist for the amputees who hobbled in on all sorts of makeshift limbs or carrying devices. There was no protocol to register or orient them.

We asked Mai to accept the position and told her she could live at the AFSC house, where there were extra rooms for employees in situations like hers. Since the house was a half mile from the Center, Mai arranged to get rides with another employee. Mai had revealed nothing about her personal life. We didn't know if she had a husband, family, or prior occupation or the location where she was injured. We hired her solely based on her attitude and intelligence.

After Mai started living at the AFSC house, we saw each other constantly. She and I worked in the large main room of the Rehab Center, where my daily routine was to oversee the activity there. On one side was a long bench where patients waited for prosthetists to create their legs or arms. Another area was full of carpentry benches and tools. A patient could watch as the prosthetist placed a new leg in a vice and trimmed a small slice or adjusted the molded top to fit around the stump. The patient would try on the leg, the prosthetists would make adjustments, and the process went on until there was a comfortable and successful fit. For the patient, it was like trying on a pair of shoes. Sitting, putting on the leg, standing to test it, taking a few steps. Repeat.

Even as I watched over the main room, I kept an eye on pediatric patients. They preferred to wait outside on the walkway shaded by a corrugated metal roof. There, they played a Vietnamese version of marbles, using small balls of dry mud. The goal was to propel the balls, using a rubber band, into the concentric circles drawn in chalk. The children stretched and released the elastics, trying to hit the balls hard enough and, with ample skill, move them toward the circle's center.

Elastic King

My favorite patient, the "Elastic King," was a seven-year-old boy who had lost both legs, one below the knee and the other above, and one eye. Elastic King had won so frequently, he had a thick woven elastic necklace. He sometimes cheated but had the advantage of experience since he had been at the Rehab Center longer than most. After all, he had two prostheses to be fitted.

When I lived on Capitol Hill in Washington, DC, years after returning from Vietnam, I compulsively collected elastic bands I found on the sidewalk. They were used to bind free advertising circulars tossed at doorsteps, and neighbors pulled the ads and coupons out and dropped the bands. It's been fifty years since I watched Elastic King play, but every elastic band still reminds me of him. And I still retrieve them from places where they have been abandoned.

As the receptionist, Mai served as the gatekeeper. Anyone entering or exiting the building checked with her. I always stopped to speak with her when I came in and multiple times during the day to answer questions about current patients or follow up on others. Mai was an astute observer. I began to respect her observations and oblique suggestions of issues to consider. In the true Vietnamese fashion, no topic was raised directly.

Mai became the all-seeing member of our team. She monitored staff dynamics, fielded questions from a range of people, updated the families of patients staying at the Center, and talked to families with patients arriving from outlying hamlets. What I didn't realize at the time was that Mai was also reporting to her contacts in the NLF. Someone else in her place near the open door might have been bothered by the heat or chilled in the rainy season, but this witty young woman with the dimpled smile was too sharp for that. She sat on her throne and became wiser and more indispensable to me and the Center every day.

Mai and I liked each other immediately, and she became not just an employee but my friend. Mai was given one of the extra rooms at the Quaker house, which were reserved for any of the AFSC Vietnamese employees who had lost their home or needed to spend a night when fighting near their village made it too dangerous for them to go home. We spent hours talking after work, often sitting on Mai's bed.

Picture of Mai and Jane 1970

Mai and I often started our conversations by holding hands. I had become used to this close physical contact with other Vietnamese women. The contact lessened my inhibitions speaking Vietnamese.

Before long, as our conversations became more animated, holding hands didn't work. Mai was skilled at using hand gestures to communicate with me. She would hold up her index finger and shake it a little, which meant she was about to make a point. As she spoke, she watched for me to nod my head—the indication that I was following. Sometimes she lightly smacked my thigh to emphasize a point. Mai's facial expressions and hand gestures helped me understand what she was saying.

Sometimes Mai was planting a seed. She had a way of introducing an idea so it would percolate in my mind. For example, she made me question why we didn't have female prosthetists. Perhaps because Confucian influence in Vietnamese culture held men as more worthy than women? Some of my Vietnamese female friends said joining the NLF was appealing because its policy was to treat men and women equally. It only seemed logical that AFSC staff should consider hiring former female patients and training them as prosthetists.

Another reason for gender disparity might be because AFSC had recruited a series of British prosthetists who were old school. It might not have occurred to them to train Vietnamese women. Many female patients had endured backbreaking labor in the rice fields before their injuries and were certainly capable of the physical work required of a prosthetist. Women are innately able to offer sympathy and often better able to encourage or scold, solicit feedback, absorb more about a patient's life story, and anticipate the anxieties of returning home with a prosthesis or wheelchair. Not only did AFSC begin to train female prosthetists but also female social workers through a program I initiated not long after the realization seeded by Mai.

Mai was interested in the differences between the US military and pacifist Quakers. She was also curious about why AFSC treated civilians from both sides of the conflict. "Does AFSC only communicate with the South Vietnamese side, or do you also talk to the National Liberation Front and the North Vietnamese?" Mai asked one day. It was an easy question, even though I had to search for the vocabulary to explain. I was familiar with medical terms and words for food, but I stumbled as I tried to express how AFSC sought to balance its work in South Vietnam by aiding all sides of the conflict. I told Mai the US Treasury Department had refused AFSC a permit to send medical or school provisions to North Vietnam or other sides of the conflict. The AFSC project in Quảng Ngãi, South Vietnam, was the only humanitarian effort in Vietnam, though AFSC continued to seek avenues to aid civilians in the north and areas under NLF control.

CHAPTER 3

Mai's Story

I told Mai about my life, family, and dreams. But it took time for her to share details of her existence during those years before we met. Why? She was the enemy my country wanted to kill.

I could not share my story. I was "the enemy," a member of the NLF. I was a revolutionary fighting for the independence of my country. Sometimes I had a gun, but I never killed anyone. My role was to use my education and persuasive voice to win support from the Vietnamese population to join our struggle.

In time I learned Mai came from a dedicated revolutionary family and lived among villages with a strong tradition of resistance to foreign powers. Mai's father, a teacher, had been offered a job working for the French colonists at the post office. Instead, he joined the Viet Minh, an independence movement founded in 1941. He fought against the French and subsequent puppet governments. His unit was assigned to the dangerous central highlands, mostly around Ban Me Tuot. Later he was arrested by the South Vietnamese government—and disappeared. Mai never heard from him again. This was not uncommon. Thousands of Vietnamese soldiers fighting for the NLF, North Vietnamese Army, and even ARVN were missing in action (MIA).

Mai's family had land near the city of Tam Ky in Quang Nam

Province, northeast of Quảng Ngãi Province, but it was not fertile. Life under French rule was dire. Rice farmers were arbitrarily imprisoned and killed if the French suspected they were helping the Viet Minh. Farmers also faced burdensome taxes, as if they were indentured to the French. Mai's uncle, brother, brother-in-law, and oldest brother's son all fought against the French and Americans and were killed. Another brother was imprisoned at Con Son Island, site of the brutal "tiger cages," concrete underground cells—too small to stand up in—where people were confined.

Mai's mother was illiterate but insisted that Mai learn to read and write by having her attend a grammar school near their home until grade seven. In middle school, Mai met a classmate from another commune, Ninh Ngoc Cu, who became her boyfriend and, a few years later, her fiancé.[8] Because of his family's revolutionary background and sympathy for a free and independent Vietnam, Cu could be swept up in a random arrest at any time. He chose to study at the local Catholic high school, thinking he might fool people into believing he was anti-Communist. Most Catholics were aligned with the South Vietnamese government, particularly those who fled south when Vietnam was temporarily divided by the 1954 Geneva Accords. This dramatic upheaval contributed to their intense anti-Communist prejudices.

Cu was a student activist and wasn't involved in serious anti-government activity, but Mai said that didn't stop the police from detaining him on September 1, 1961.

> The government police came right into his classroom, grabbed him from his desk, tied him up, and took him forcefully out of the room. The government of the Republic of South Vietnam had no hesitation using intimidating tactics on the civilian population. Like my father, Cu abruptly, mysteriously disappeared. My conviction was that the South Vietnamese government killed Cu to prevent him

---
8   In Vietnam in the 1960s, formal engagement is akin to taking marriage vows.

from joining his father and two brothers, loyal Communist Party members who had joined the NLF to fight against the Americans in 1965.

Mai mourned Cu. She had believed they would spend their lives together in their village. Cu's mother and Mai never recovered his body, compounding their distress. Most Vietnamese believe the souls of loved ones live on after death. Ancestral worship involves elaborate rituals to connect the deceased to an afterlife with other ancestors while maintaining a strong bond with the living. If the deceased does not have a proper burial in an ancestral grave, their soul will wander, becoming a "homeless ghost." Mai agonized over not recovering Cu's body for the family and community to honor him. She developed chest pains that led to difficulty breathing—panic attacks—and began to see apparitions. Her fiancé's ghost appeared as an image in her room and in the sky and trees when she looked outside.

> The visits increased and got worse, I felt as if I was going mad, and my family asked a shaman to visit me to calm the ghost. We asked this person with clairvoyant powers to help find Cu's body, but only a bullet turned up. And it could have belonged to anyone.

Joining the National Liberation Front

Because Mai and Cu had talked incessantly about the injustices and cruelty of the South Vietnamese government and American aggressors, their shared revolutionary spirit was strong. Mai wanted to leave her village and join the NLF immediately to avenge the loss of her fiancé.

> The Americans had killed my love and were destroying my country. I applied to go to the mountains directly, but the NLF made me wait two years. During that time, I acted as an

NLF courier, carrying documents between locations. Finally, in 1964, I arranged to join.

It was best if people left one by one to join the Front since it would draw less attention than if several people left at once. A female friend, Cat, and I left together. We walked for one day and met up with eight young men, slightly older than us. Only three of the ten of us are still alive.

Mai was chosen to train as a teacher. She traveled on foot for a month and a half through the mountains and jungles of Quang Nam province. Occasionally, bombs dropped close to Mai's small group. Mai's equipment included a walking stick, backpack, mosquito netting, and hammock. Mai laughed when she told me how her sandals caused blisters.

There weren't any stores in the jungle to buy replacements, so I had no option but to walk on. Sometimes one of the men in my group would help carry my knapsack because, in the beginning, sores appeared even on my shoulders. I needed time for the skin to toughen up, but as a woman, I needed to be independent.

Do you have an expression in English that means "learn by walking through fire"? Well, during the hike through the mountains, I was very close to bomb strikes that were terrifying. I'd never been near a direct bomb hit when I lived at home, but during the one and a half months of walking, we would hear artillery fire and bombs that were frighteningly close. We'd have to change direction or just stop walking and hide.

Honestly, I was frightened. What kept my spirits up were the camaraderie and friendship of us undergoing these hardships together. The joy of those times stemmed from the shared idealism for reaching the goal of independence, liberty, and peace for Vietnam. We were all in the struggle together, and we felt energy from each other. During our hiking days, I even picked some flowers along the way, and sometimes we would sing revolutionary songs.

One time we had to hike at night. Each of us had a jar of fireflies hitched to our backpacks. The flickering light led the way for the person following, like miniature stars captured to lead us. We were young people, on our own, following the dream of serving our country. We were proud and happy. Even with the danger of being killed, we were idealistic and optimistic. Those years were the happiest days of my life. The intense comradery replaced the absence of family, and we all felt motivated by our ideals.

Finally, we reached our destination, where we would attend training in various subjects. There was a senior man and woman in charge who talked to us about our interests and emphasized that we had chosen to join voluntarily and could go home anytime. The NLF would help arrange for us to return home if we regretted our choice. For six months, I studied how to teach children in the fifth and sixth grades. I was trained in educational methodology and specialized course content, like math and Vietnamese literature.

After my training, I left for my assigned school in the Dat Tho District in Binh Dinh Province, just south of the province of Quảng Ngãi, which was a two-to-three-day walk. The first time I taught for ninety minutes straight, my voice got dry, and my legs ached. I might have been slightly tired, but I was very proud I'd joined the revolution and was being useful. During the day, we teachers worked with our pupils to grow crops, and at night we taught them in school. My students ranged in age from seven to twelve. I loved them like family. They remained respectful of me as their teacher and didn't take advantage of my affection.

We didn't have a school building because the Americans

would've bombed it. Instead, we taught in different houses or even outside. When bombing started, we would all run to hide in shelters or tunnels. Sometimes the children came with me, and we moved to another village. Bombing, move, stay, and teach. Bombing, move, stay, and teach. That was the rhythm of my days. One time a bomb dropped directly on a shelter holding my pupils. Eleven were killed immediately; one died the next day. Only two lived. It was a scar on my heart. We were filled with patriotic feelings, but this awful incident and other close calls reminded us daily that we were living under dangerous and dire conditions. Children are innocent. I recognized my life was in danger, but I mainly thought of my comrades and my sweet pupils.

Newspaper Work

For many months, Mai only told me about her work as a teacher and how she then progressed to being a coach and manager.

I advanced to monitoring other teachers to maintain quality. If a teacher didn't meet the standards, I would encourage and help that teacher become a better professional.

A year later, I was invited to be on the team of people who produced a newspaper in the liberated zone. It was a fascinating job. I listened to reports of battles and progress of the war from different radio programs and summarized the news. We may also add some poetry. An older person with more experience would read and edit my work until I advanced enough to work independently. We didn't have a printing machine, just a lithography stone and ink. I had to carry the stone everywhere we went, every time we moved. I was exposed to literature by famous Vietnamese authors, like Nguyen Trai and Nguyen Dinh Tri, and the poet To Huu, and I learned about Vietnamese heroes and successes during the French and American wars. I was gaining a wider picture of the war, learning about battles and struggles in other areas of Vietnam, not just in my local area. I also prepared materials for an upcoming surprise offensive planned for January 1969.

Tam Ky Attack—and Public Relations (Propaganda) Work

All over Vietnam, there were more than forty attacks planned for different provincial capitals at the time of the Lunar New Year in 1969. I was intimately involved with the NLF unit that planned and executed an attack on Tam Ky at Tet, the time when we celebrate our Lunar New Year. There was a regiment of North Vietnamese troops joining us.

We called it the Uprising of Tet Mau Tan.[9] An ethnic group acted as local guides as we made our way from the mountains to the city. In the mountains, we wore our revolutionary hats and clothes, but when we got to the town of Tam Ky, the tribal people had prepared different clothes so that we looked like the local city people living in South Vietnam-controlled areas.

We went into the city around 4 p.m. to be prepared for the attack that was planned for 1 a.m., when the new year, the Year of the Goat, began. I hid in a big stack of straw at dusk, waiting for the night. My comrades had guns, but I was going to have the honor of announcing the liberation on the radio, so I only had a paper with my speech. We attacked strategic places in the city and held the ARVN military base on a hill for a while. The fighting was fierce. ARVN and the US countered with artillery and effective air strikes. Neither we, the NLF, nor the North Vietnamese had any planes. We were forced to pull back. The local minority people helped me and other NLF soldiers get safely back to the mountains. My close friend, Son, just fifteen years old, and an eighteen-year-old

---

9   Year of the Monkey.

cousin were killed. I heard later that nearly 500 North Vietnamese and NLF soldiers were killed.

The failure of the Tet attack on Tam Ky was a huge disappointment. Of course, it showed that the NLF and North Vietnamese troops[10] were strong and supported by the population to such an extent that we could launch an attack in Tam Ky, as we did in many other provincial capitals. In Hue, the NLF and North Vietnamese were driven back too, but at least they held the city for twenty-four days before they retreated. The battle for Hue was considered the major turning point of the war for the American military, but to me, not having success at my local level was agonizing. We knew, though, that gaining freedom for Vietnam was a long-term battle.

We regrouped after the attack on Tam Ky and assessed our strengths. Many city people in Tam Ky favored the NLF, but they were prisoners of the Americans and ARVN, who were in control of the city. We were fighting a guerilla war against a heavily armed enemy with superior military equipment and plans. So, the decision was made that we should focus on the base of our support, the country farmers who were being held in "strategic hamlets." The South Vietnamese government forced people off their land and into hamlets surrounded by barbed wire fencing. The government thought the Strategic Hamlet Program, a policy of separating the people from the land, would prevent them from supporting the NLF. Farmers were held in mini prisons to prevent them from getting supplies or food to the guerillas and to prevent the NLF from recruiting men and women to join the liberation struggle. But the populations resented being taken off their land, often placed in hot army supply tents and eating imported Texas rice. They were prevented from carrying on their major

---

10 North Vietnamese soldiers were called the People's Army of Vietnam (PAV) or North Vietnamese Army (NVA)

life-supporting occupation: growing and harvesting rice. The US had so little understanding of the heartbeat of our country.

I was part of an NLF team, usually three of us, who would make surprise visits to these hamlets at night. True, they were guarded by the ARVN, but these soldiers were oftentimes distracted, sleeping, or lazy. We usually could enter the hamlet without a problem. If they shot at us, we would have to shoot back, but I wasn't trained as a soldier, so I didn't have a gun.

My real job was to talk to the people. I was an expert at propaganda. I wasn't brainwashing people with political slogans; I was just talking sense to them. When they were sleeping, we'd wake them up and say, "Please get up and listen to us." We urged them to go back to their villages and work in the fields to pass on the knowledge of growing and harvesting rice to the younger generation. We encouraged them, asking, "How are your children and grandchildren going to survive if they don't know how to grow rice? You know Vietnam was the largest exporter of rice in the world before the American war, and now you are fed bags of old, broken pieces of American rice kernels. Remember all the fruits and vegetables from before the war, the hundreds of different kinds of bananas? And flowers? And the peacefulness of our villages? We need to till the earth and return to these treasures of our land. Your ancestors are buried on your land. Go be with them. It will be better and more comfortable in your village."

I have had similar experiences when talking to refugees in strategic hamlets or in the big refugee camp along the river in Quảng Ngãi. They would make the war seem so insane and their demands so simple. Farmers wanted to go back to their land, where they had buried their ancestors and harvested the rice that provided their livelihood. They said, "Tell the US government, we want to live in our own country with no foreign occupiers interfering."

I was so good at talking to people that sometimes they would cry. Why? Because I reached into their hearts and said out loud what they were thinking. When we suggested that they destroy the enclosures where they were held hostage, it was what they truly wanted to do. We also gave them information about the successes of the NLF, information they did not get from the ARVN radio stations or newspapers. We encouraged them with Uncle Ho[11] words so they understood the direction of the revolution, and we reminded them of their own longing to be independent of foreign powers and to be able to return home to their ancestral land. We were trying our best, with all our mind and resources.

One time I was in a strategic hamlet and saw a soldier sleeping with three grenades at the head of his bed. He was so startled to see me, a woman with a rifle (sometimes I did have a gun) standing near his bed, that he just jumped up and ran away. I picked up the grenades and said, "Oh luu dan bay" ("Oh, a flying bullet"), and handed the grenades to another female cadre who was with me.

This public relations work could be dangerous. We could accidentally step on a mine or be captured or killed when we tried to enter the hamlets. One of my friends from the mountains worked as a liaison between the NLF soldiers in liberated zones and NLF contacts in the city. He was captured and tortured while I was still in the mountains, but despite almost dying of torture, he did not confess my name or location to anyone.

These were not easy times. We were all hungry. The Americans were spraying Agent Orange on us, on our land.

---

11 Ho Chi Minh was the founder of the revolutionary movement for an independent Vietnam, free of colonial powers. Ho Chi Minh served as the president of the Democratic Republic of Vietnam (North Vietnam) from 1945 until his death in 1969. He was affectionately known as "Uncle Ho."

Once, when the planes were spraying us, I was able to find a piece of nylon to cover myself to keep the spray from touching my skin. Other times, I couldn't avoid getting wet. The poison was killing the vegetation, and we were forced to eat what was below ground. We cut the roots of the banana tree. The plant might be dead and have turned yellow on top, but we cut the roots. Jackfruit too. We made them into two different dishes. One dish was root mixed with rice, and the other was a side dish made from the roots.

Mai Loses Her Legs

Those years must have been so painful for Mai—for her body and spirit—and I wondered if it was hard for her to talk about them. I loved her like a sister and wanted her to know I was sorry that my country was responsible. We had never talked about these cruel days.

During those years between 1968 and 1971, it is true that we were having a harder time moving around as freely as before because of the increased American presence in the region. The fighting was going on all the time, but we mostly practiced "let" (translation: fade back, melt away) by not engaging in fighting. The Americans would come into our territory and conduct operations. Our understanding of how the Americans operated their war was that if the helicopter released the troops here, one hour later, the troops would be at this specific point, and then an hour later, here. We could usually predict their movements.

As Mai came closer to describing how she lost her legs, she drew pictures with her finger, indicating locations. She emphatically marked each point, with animation and anger, as she reached the climax of her story.

We kept careful watch on where the Americans were operating. We didn't provoke them. For the most part, we left them alone. We focused on organizing the people. I had already been working with my good friend, Cat, from 1969 to 1970. For the first three months, we were working at the district level, but then we were promoted to the provincial level. Although Cat was a nurse with specialized nursing training, she leaned on me for help in strengthening her reading and writing abilities. We were like lost sisters and remain close to this day. There were many near-death experiences that bonded us.

Cat had been promoted to the chairman of the Women's Union in the district of Quang Nam, and I was elected vice chairman. In preparation for the celebration of International Women's Day, we held an organizational meeting in Que Son. At the meeting, each of us took separate responsibility for different areas and projects. We walked to a fork in the path, and Cat said to me, "Goodbye, my friend. Now you will go that way, and I will go this way."

It was 1971, either the third or fourth day of March. We'd been warned that the Americans were in the area, and I knew they had arrived because I saw their helicopter. But I calculated their distance and was sure they weren't close. I just didn't expect them to attack so fast. Sometimes local people were bribed by Vietnamese interpreters to inform on us, and someone must have exposed our location, saying, "Those Communists will have a meeting near here." Usually, the Americans plodded like heavy water buffalo. Since I hadn't heard any noise, I was planning to climb a tree to see if I could spot the soldiers before I went further.

The meeting started at noon, but it was now about 4 p.m. I walked up to the tree that I planned to climb and triggered an American Claymore mine. There was grass all around, and I didn't see the mine until I heard "bam, bam," then a flash like a crack of lightning blazing in front of my eyes. I heard more "bams" as my body was lifted up and then dropped down on the ground. There were two more explosions nearby. I didn't know I was injured. My natural reaction was to stand up, but I couldn't. It was a surreal sensation to want my body to follow my brain, but it wouldn't. Then I knew I was injured.

At first, I was still conscious, but I couldn't open my eyes because it was so bright. When I was able to look, I could see that my right leg looked whole. There was blood and tissue, but my foot was still attached to my leg. But the left leg was mangled, smashed, and bloody, and my foot was missing. I could see parts of it in the grass. I touched my head to feel my face. I felt flesh stuck to my cheek. I kept thinking, *It was a mine. It was a mine.* The words of a superior flashed through my mind: "Sometimes the end can come while going about a routine activity or while fighting. Just suddenly. Death can be as normal as eating a meal." Then I went unconscious.

I was injured by a mine, printed with the words, "Front Toward Enemy," which I couldn't read because I didn't understand English, but I had been told about them. Mines like this were made in a green plastic convex shape designed to deliver the optimum distribution of 700 steel balls into the person in front of the mine. Claymore mines were grim killers.

I hadn't seen the mine, but it was probably manually detonated by an American soldier hiding. Ironically, the American soldiers on this same operation, who had laid the mines, saved my life. They called in a helicopter to medivac me, this captured enemy person, to the closest military hospital.

I was very cold because my blood was running out and there were strong winds from the blades of the helicopter.

I heard the sound of scissors cutting my clothes. My hair had been combed into two plaits, but now it was filled with pieces of my body. One of the Vietnamese soldiers with the American military unit said, "This bitch is Communist, pure Communist. Let's cut off her other leg to stop her from going anywhere. Then she can crawl to work."

I was taken to the American Marine-operated hospital at Chu Lai.

At first, I didn't even know where I was. When I regained consciousness, my legs were already cut off, one below the knee and one above. I wondered if they had deliberately cut my intact leg above the knee, as the Vietnamese interpreter had suggested, to make me crawl for the rest of my life. I also had an incision across my abdomen. This frightened me because I hadn't even realized I'd had surgery on my stomach. But since Claymore mines shoot steel pellets, some of them must have ripped open my stomach. There was a big scar and plastic tubes going from my stomach to a machine beside the bed. No one ever explained the surgical cut across my belly. The hospital lights were on all the time, so I didn't know if it was day or night. The mattress was white, oh, so white.

Weights were attached to my legs—a ten-kilogram weight to one and a five-kilogram weight to the other—to try to force my legs to be straight. My arms were connected to plastic lines. I had one in a nostril with liquid flowing through it. When I opened my eyes, I saw two American Military Police sitting beside my bed. I knew this meant I was a prisoner of war.

My hospital room was only for prisoners of war. There were twenty-five people occupying the rows of beds. For the first time, I saw American women—they were nurses.

One day I was able to talk to a young Vietnamese soldier, seventeen years old, who told me, "I was in the

North Vietnamese Army, and the Americans attacked us in Quang Tri."

That information was staggering. His words were good news—verification of serious fighting happening at the DMZ, the dividing line between North and South Vietnam.

Once, when I was sleeping in a drugged stupor, I opened my eyes to see a hand with golden hair on the arm. The voice connected to the hand was saying, "VC, VC" (Viet Cong). I knew it was an American, but I couldn't see clearly, only enough to know that he was slipping my twenty-four-karat gold ring off my finger. Let me explain why this ring was important. When someone joined the NLF, they would be categorized with two definitions: thoat ly or semi-thoat ly. A person who was called semi thoat ly was supporting the NLF but still living in their village. But, in my case, I was a thoat ly, which meant I had given up living at home and was totally committed—full-time, not semi or part-time—to living and working in zones—mountains or jungles—controlled by the NLF.

No matter how poor a family was, families tried to give some taels[12] of gold to the soldiers in their families in case of illness or need. As a provincial official, I was expected to provide food and medicine for myself for six months. The ring could have been used in case I couldn't grow enough food to feed myself. I was sad to lose this token of sacrifice and money from my mother.

The Americans interrogated me many times. There was often a Vietnamese interpreter next to my bed. He had a Saigon accent, knelt on the floor, and put his mouth right close to my ear. An American soldier stood beside him while the interpreter asked, "What is your name? Where are you from?" I had forged papers with a false name, Nguyen thi Mai. I said I was from a

---

12 A *tael* is a traditional unit measurement of gold. The term was used in East and Southeast Asia. In 1959 China standardized a tael as 50 grams of gold.

faraway village. I told him I was just a farmer. They thought I might be a Communist because I was wearing a tai beo, not a conical hat, when I was captured. What they didn't understand was that in the area where I was injured, Communists and farmers alike wore tai beo hats. The Americans were ignorant of most of the customs of our people.

How long was Mai at Chu Lai? Sometimes I took patients there to see if American military doctors could help us with a diagnosis or treatment. Of course, I didn't go into the POW ward, but it would have been coincidental if we had met there!

Transfer to Quảng Ngãi

I lost track of time at Chu Lai, and I am not sure how long I was there. Then one day a couple of patients, including me, were loaded into a helicopter. It flew along the coastline, avoiding the trees leading toward the mountains. I thought, *The NLF must control the mountains and land adjacent to the coast, and the only area safe for them to fly is out over the ocean.* That day, there was a pilot, a soldier with a mounted machine gun, and a few patients in the helicopter. I was head to toe with another person on a stretcher, an older man who was probably a POW like me. He whispered to me, "Remove your tag."

I looked down and could see there was a tag tied to me with plastic string with the words, "VC POW." It seemed as if it would take forever to chew through the string, but I was able to do it, and the old man threw the tag out the open door that looked out over the sea.

Communicating with the NLF

Mai's life changed after she became an AFSC employee. The 10 p.m. curfew in Quảng Ngãi gave us many hours in the evening to work or talk. Through our conversations, Mai decided to trust me. Now she was going to test me. Mai suggested I communicate with the NLF. She told me the AFSC Rehabilitation Center's work was fairly well known in the region, mainly because patients who returned to their villages talked about how the Center provided prostheses at no cost and remarked on the Quakers unusual pacifist position of treating any war casualty.

Mai argued that AFSC should explain its work and philosophy to higher-ups in NLF forces rather than just relying on recognition among the farming population. Mai was right. The Rehab Center might be known locally, but if North Vietnamese troops were to come into the province, they would not necessarily have any information about us. It would be useful to be known as a humanitarian organization that was neutral in the conflict.

The dividing lines between NLF-and ARVN-held territories were ambiguous. Most South Vietnamese did not refer to areas controlled by the NLF as "liberated zones" or "Communist territories." Rather, the Vietnamese used the term *e dang kia,* which means "on the other side." It seemed like a subtle way to acknowledge Vietnam as one country, one people, even during war.

"A woman sweeping her doorway on one side of the street might be giving food to NLF guerillas, who would silently come to her home at night. The man sitting in his doorway across the street smoking a cigarette might be a member of the CIA-backed Phoenix Program."[13] The program's mission was "to identify and destroy via infiltrations, torture, capture, terrorism, counterterrorism, interrogation, and killings" those suspected of working with the NLF.[14] Most of us referred to the Phoenix Program as "the civilian assassination program" since CIA intelligence on its targets was often wrong, and many innocent people were assassinated. Part of what made my adrenalin spike was the constant game of trying to decipher where it was safe to walk, who

---

13 Frances FitzGerald, *The New Yorker,* July 2, 1972, page 13.
14 Wikepedia. https://en.wikipedia.org/wiki/Phoenix_Program

was lying, who was truthful, and who might be an agent or double agent. Nothing was clear. Having some "protection" from the NLF or North Vietnamese, if their soldiers came into Quảng Ngãi, might be a way to keep the AFSC program safe.

I conjured up a mental picture of mailing a letter to the NLF or making a phone call to the jungle using two tin cans tied to either end of a long string. I waited for Mai's instructions. She asked me to find a thin piece of paper and compose a paragraph in Vietnamese about AFSC's philosophy and work. Then, in the smallest script possible, I wrote on the two-by-three-inch paper. I watched as Mai rolled the paper into a narrow tube shape, smaller than a pipe cleaner. She wrapped it in plastic and lit a match to melt the edges, sealing it from any water damage.

Mai described how the note would get from her to an NLF official. It would be passed to a vendor at the market and placed inside a small fish. The fish would be sold to a designated person who used a code word. It would be put in the market basket of the purchaser and then passed, once or twice, among various women until it was taken into the jungle.

Crossing the border of an area controlled by the Americans to an area controlled by the NLF was dangerous, especially when carrying food or supplies. There was little traffic over the forbidden buffer between the two sides. Somehow my message reached "the other side." Though there was a risk, Mai assured me that, so far, no fish had ever been confiscated, especially if it was small and not worthy of an ARVN soldier stealing it. Mai laughed and said, "Fish aren't an item ARVN soldiers want. They are challenging to keep from stinking and spoiling in a hot climate like ours."

Mai explained that before the war had taken its toll, when more hens and eggs were available, she slid a message into a hole in an empty egg and placed the egg among others in a basket. Now, anyone carrying a basket of eggs was suspected of being rich and susceptible to bribes and abuse. There were other ingenious ways to get messages from the American and South Vietnamese zone to jungles and mountains, but this time it would be via the "fish method."

It was three months before I received a return note saying "Uncle Nam" appreciated my letter and hoped AFSC work would continue successfully and safely treat all the people of Vietnam. Two more letters were exchanged. I hoped they would ensure AFSC operations and employees could continue—safely—no matter what happened.

CHAPTER 4

Evacuate Now!
1972–1973

In late January 1972, approaching the Lunar New Year, the fighting was violent around Quảng Ngãi. American troops began to withdraw, and ARVN and South Korean troops around Quảng Ngãi feared the dedicated, driven, and committed enemy. ARVN didn't want to meet the guerillas "face to face," and South Koreans, soldiers whose salaries and weaponry were paid for by the US, massacred entire villages to warn the NLF to stay away.[15] The air buzzed with Huey helicopters, tanks rumbled down streets, and at night there was continuous artillery and mortar fire. The sky lit up in flashes of pink from flares, and there was an eerie sense of doom.

Patients missing limbs arrived daily. Was the fighting building to a repeat of the 1968 Tet Offensive? It might have been the case when, a few months later, two military officers pulled up to the Quaker house in a Jeep. I could see them through the open door. One officer remained in the vehicle; the other stepped out. His jungle-patterned uniform was dark green from sweat. He didn't leap out of his Jeep the way military men did in World War II movies. He moved slowly; he was clearly suffering in the heat.

Entering the kitchen, he stood awkwardly as he stared at the Quaker team, a group of women and men in Vietnamese- style clothing sitting around a table with rice bowls and chopsticks. We invited him

---

15 Summers, John, *Boston Globe*, "The Biggest Vietnam War Story that Americans Don't Want to Talk About," August 2023.

to sit, but he demurred and asked to speak to "your leader," as if we were an exotic tribe. I could have explained that we used consensus to make decisions, and there wasn't a leader in the ranked military sense—we had "directors"—but there wasn't time.

I stood up from the table and asked the officer into our team living room. He was uncomfortable, his eyes fixed on a small yellow pillow in a chair. He didn't make eye contact with me. His message was short: "The Viet Cong have surrounded the city and hold most of the province. You must evacuate immediately. I am here to deliver the message that the US military is willing to fly you to safety in the next twenty-four hours. The ideal time would be to leave early tomorrow morning if we aren't overrun tonight."

I shared the news with the team. We began deliberating over the startling news to reach consensus. Quaker consensus is a process of seeking "a way forward, forging a mutual agreement that respects every person's feeling and opinion." We could not find consensus that night and missed being evacuated in the morning. We all shared responsibility to the Vietnamese staff and patients. Those most adamant about refusing to evacuate were the medically trained staff. They had come to teach and had close relationships with their Vietnamese students. These team members felt it would be patronizing, even racist, to come to "do good" but take off when things got heated. Others argued that if we were injured or hurt, we would put additional pressure on the Vietnamese staff. An attempt to evacuate us during fighting could endanger Vietnamese or rescuers' lives. Or, if we were to become ill while sheltering in the NLF-controlled mountain areas until fighting abated, the Vietnamese might feel compelled to use their precious medicine to heal us.[16] We could consume food already scarce in liberated areas. We might get sick from drinking unpurified water. As

---

16 This had been the case with AFSC doctor Marge Nelson when she was captured in Hue in 1968 during Tet and taken to the mountains in Laos. NLF soldiers gave her scarce and valuable antibiotics, and her Vietnamese captors donated condensed milk, powdered eggs, and sugar because they wanted her to "get strong and healthy." Marjorie Nelson, *To Live in Peace*, self-published, p. 380.

Westerners, we had little resistance to some illnesses. Team members had been ill with dengue fever, malaria, and typhoid, among others. If we became seriously incapacitated, we could be putting the burden of our care on our Vietnamese friends.

For example, I lacked resistance to certain bacteria, causing boils on my skin. The boils swelled into lumps on my neck and face. My problem was external and a vanity, not actually debilitating, so I didn't complain. I also remembered a bout with typhoid during my first weeks in Vietnam and knew what it was like to be soaked with fever. It took days before I could walk. What if this happened when we left Quảng Ngãi and headed to the safety of the mountains? The rest of the team would have to leave me.

We kept "to-go" bags by our beds. Mine held a toothbrush, a postcard of the Isenheim Altarpiece in Colmar, France, a pen, and a small keychain fob woven by the mother of one of my favorite students, no key attached. The fob was made from a piece of twine that had bundled newspapers for his delivery route. I had brought no pictures of my parents and brother to Vietnam. This wasn't the case for NLF soldiers. Family photos were often the only items found on the bodies of dead guerillas. The American provincial advisor proudly displayed sentimental items belonging to a dead NLF soldier on his office walls: photos of his fiancée and a tiny NLF flag.

Now, our "to-go" bags were no longer theoretical.

Conversation with Mai

Before going to bed, I sat on the stairs leading to the second floor, alone with my feelings. And then I saw Mai walking toward me, using her right hand to place her crutch in front of her, a body on stilts, high up with no legs. When Mai had started to learn to walk again, she admitted how afraid she was and nervous she would topple over.

Mai let me help her sit, and she moved my hand to her leg, patting it. The physical contact was welcome. She looked into my eyes, and we talked about the situation. Mai said with absolute assurance, "You will be all right. We can get to the mountains and escape. You will be fine." I wanted to cry out, *"No, no! You don't understand! You are not 'fine,' so how can you say I will be?"* It shocked me to realize Mai considered herself "fine" even though she had no legs. I was afraid to lose my legs. Her definition of being okay was different than mine.

Images of skiing flashed in my mind—my knees and upper body lifting as I maneuvered around a course, my skis at the top of a mogul, creating a spray of bright, almost blinding, white snow on a brilliant day—vivid mental pictures of my family's annual trip to New Hampshire. Oh, how free it would feel to move down the slopes again.

I'm not sure why winter images came before spring, memories of that slightly scratchy feel of a linen dress, walking in high heels, a sweater over my shoulders. Then my thoughts jumped to the summer smell of balsam trees in Maine, picking wild blueberries and rose hips. I needed my legs to feel whole.

The outcome of our team discussion was this: most would stay. I would travel to Saigon, let the home office in Philadelphia know we were all right, and continue our mission. The home office was legitimately worried. They sent a cable to the Rehabilitation Center, requesting that David follow me to Saigon and then we would travel to Philadelphia to discuss the situation in-person before going to France. In Paris, we were directed to contact the North and the Provisional Revolutionary Government (PRG),[17] the Vietnamese diplomatic delegations, already in France for the Paris Peace Talks.

It was an uncertain time. The strategy of the North and PRG was twofold: to engage in diplomatic measures through the talks and to increase military pressure in Vietnam. That was why fighting increased around Quảng Ngãi, although Henry Kissinger, at a news conference in October 1972, had stated, "Peace is at hand." By December, Nixon unleashed the "Christmas Bombing," dropping more than two

---

17 The PRG was founded in 1969. It incorporated the NLF and negotiated at the Paris Peace Talks.

thousand tons of bombs on the cities of Hanoi and Haiphong. It was January 1973, and the future was hard to predict.

David and I left Quảng Ngãi and flew around the world in two weeks.

Paris

In Paris, it was as if color had been added to a black-and-white film: a peaceful place with wide, paved streets and sidewalks, lined with crowded cafés, where people strolled in orderly fashion. I felt giddy. David and I had both spent time in France; he had studied at French universities. We loved the French people and food. There were no sounds of gunfire, no maimed bodies, no dust rising from the streets. None of the oppressive heat.

There was a North Vietnamese embassy in Paris, and the PRG had official representation in a modest structure in another part of the city, Verrieres-le-Buisson. AFSC intended to remain in Vietnam. David and I were given the goal of conveying and reinforcing the message that AFSC was a pacifist organization in Vietnam to serve injured Vietnamese civilians regardless of political beliefs. It intended to keep its promise to train Vietnamese staff and serve the hundreds of patients who came to our Center.

It was uplifting to meet with the Vietnamese delegations. They were amazed we spoke Vietnamese. North Vietnamese delegates spoke with an accent different from the central coastal speech. There was a thorough discussion of AFSC's work, and both the North Vietnamese and PRG understood our position. Some of them knew of the ship's delivery of medical supplies to North Vietnam by a Quaker Action group.[18] Other delegates referred to a Quaker, Norman Morrison, who self-immolated in protest under Secretary of State Robert McNamara's window at the Pentagon, reminiscent of the actions of some Buddhist monks.

---

18 A rogue action in 1967 captured the American media's attention: daring Quaker activists who sailed a fifty-foot boat to North Vietnam, delivering medical supplies after the US government refused to grant AFSC a license.

Having lost a sense of time, we were surprised to realize the next day was May 1, International Workers Day. Traditionally, especially around Paris, bouquets of lily of the valley are given to friends to mark the holiday. We visited Buddhist nuns associated with the NLF/PRG, and I was touched when a small nun gave me a tiny bouquet of the sweet- smelling, bell-shaped flowers. Her gentleness and strength were reminders of the character of the Vietnamese back "home" in Vietnam.

This same nun took my hand and gave me a speech on Vietnam's struggles to be independent, starting with the defeat of the Chinese to end 1,100 years of domination. In 938, a Vietnamese navy commander trapped Chinese warships in a major river near Ha Long Bay by hiding metal spikes underwater. The Chinese were lured upriver by the Vietnamese in shallow-bottomed boats and grounded as the tide receded, making them vulnerable to attack.

The nun covered a few more thousand years of history, including the American war and the fighting that had brought David and me to Paris. She declared with confidence that, of course, the Vietnamese people would rise again, and the country would be united. Her sweeping view of her country's history was common to most Vietnamese. They believed they would eventually oust the American foreign invaders, as they had done to other powers in the past.

We also met with Father Thi, a Catholic priest who was part of the Third Force.[19] A longtime resident of France, he organized speeches and meetings among the expat Vietnamese community to encourage support for a unified Vietnam and an openness to returning to Vietnam. He told them, "Your country will be needing people like you with education and skill."

Father Thi took us to a restaurant where Ho Chi Minh had washed dishes, one of his many jobs during the years he lived in France while

---

19   The Third Force was composed of individuals and groups who wanted an independent, peaceful solution to the war, separate from the NLF or South Vietnamese government. Students, several religious groups like the Buddhists, and Cao Dai comprised the Third Force movement, which held demonstrations and distributed literature.

agitating and organizing for the independence of Vietnam. Oddly, in Paris I dined on delicate and delicious samplings of Vietnamese food. So, this was what Vietnamese food tasted like! It was different from the simple fare the AFSC team ate in Quảng Ngãi, where the war had made vegetables, fruits, and meat scarce. Vietnamese cuisine in Paris was delicious and varied with layered aromas and flavors.

After two weeks in Paris, David and I returned to Vietnam.

Returning to Quảng Ngãi

We had started our trip on a prop plane from the short, single airstrip cut out of the jungle in Quảng Ngãi and traveled by massive jetliner to Hong Kong, Philadelphia, Paris, Bangkok, and Saigon. Now we were back to the single airstrip on a prop plane. I was exhausted but glad to be back with the team and the Rehabilitation Center's work.

The Center had operated as usual during the fighting, with Western and Vietnamese staff working every day. The concrete walls and corrugated tin roof held down by sandbags hadn't been damaged. No rockets had hit our house. The people around Quảng Ngãi had suffered extensive damage to their homes and land and loss of life. Our staff had been nervous, yet none of the Vietnamese or American personnel had left. In another field report, Caroline described the weeks David and I were away:

> For several days now, there's been lots to write. . . . There was a typhoon, Flossie, which lasted about three days: cut electricity and blew portions of the metal roof off the Rehab Center. On Saturday we began to hear the booms and bangs. Reports didn't tell much until we went out to the airport where we met some soldiers driving the arms-loaded Cobra helicopters, the sinister-looking black ones that carry bombs, grenades, machine guns, and more. They told us that things were heavy, and Mo Duc was getting blasted. Saturday night,

it really came alive—or deadening—the sky was on fire. We could see a flash, wait about twenty seconds, and then feel and hear the vibrations—all the way down to the gut, where it makes you want to vomit and scream—but after a while just sit and cry silently, inwardly—almost hopelessly—certainly helplessly. It started about 12 a.m.

After watching out the windows for a while, we all went down to the living room and slept together—that felt better—although it still sent a chill up and down my spine each time the bombing set up tremors that shook the ground and rattled the windows and doors. And what's to follow it all? That's the real fear, what will be revealed about the injuries and deaths of civilians—more patients—more heartache. Finally, we slept through the noises, and the next day was a bright, beautiful, blue and green Sunday morning. Nothing ever seems fair—at all.

Sunday, some of the team went to Buddha Mountain. While we were there, we watched the ARVN shell Son Tinh[20]—hearing the cruel muffled whiz overhead, after the original blast from the nearby firebase, and then the impact boom, the smoke rising, the dust and the shouts, machine guns, all of it, all on a Sunday morning . . . tired, sad, wind, blue sky, birds, bombs.

Later, we talked to McBride, the American advisor. He said VC had suffered a terrific blow (And what about the people? I thought). The US was not using any B-52s, he "didn't think"—we knew he was lying; we saw the bombs and knew an American advisor was busy in Mo Duc for the past thirty-six hours, calling in air strikes and directing the ship fire by himself. By himself? They said he was exhausted—and I didn't care if he was tired (he was probably scared too). What of those who were running, hiding, and dying—they're

---

20 My Lai is a hamlet within the district of Son Tinh.

probably tired too.[21]

We were awakened this time by blanket bombing—to us, twenty kilometers away, it felt like a long, muffled tremor—shaking me to the core. Cold sweat, heart pounding, mouth dry, thinking of them, me, us, here, them. *I don't want to die. They don't want to die. For God's sake, stop. STOP. Please make them stop, the ones driving the planes. They don't understand what they're doing—they can't. They don't know Mr. Bich—and his wife who's nine months pregnant. they don't know.*[22]

I returned to find many war-related injuries and new patients with missing limbs. Some Vietnamese staff lost their ancestral homes to B-52 bombings that eliminated all traces of their homes, temples, and cultivated land. Napalm strikes killed many and forced new burn patients into the hospital. Many of our staff were directly affected. The entire family of one paralyzed patient was killed.

When David and I returned from Paris, the staff was anxious to hear what the Vietnamese delegations had to say, and we listened as our Vietnamese employees and patients described the horrors of the past weeks. Yet, most of the talk was about the growing NLF presence, control in Quảng Ngãi Province, and speculation about how the war might end. The hottest news was the US/ARVN had captured documents from the commander of an NLF regiment, indicating the NLF was planning to attack Quảng Ngãi in ten to fifteen days. A map showed NLF troops to the south of Quảng Ngãi and mortars and soldiers in the mountains to the west—split into a battalion on each side of the river—with more to the south, east, and north. There were large numbers of soldiers, military equipment, and sapper units surrounding the city.

---

21   Caroline Elliot, Report to AFSC, October 9, 1972. Caroline wrote several letters during this tense period. Caroline died at sixty-one in her home state of North Carolina.
22   Caroline's report detailed her fondness for certain patients and staff. "If they could only know them—Cung's family, Anh Hai, Thuy's grandfather—play with them, eat in their huts, talk to them, they wouldn't, they couldn't. How can they anyway? I don't understand it, and I don't want to either. And please stop the frightened dreams."

Again, US advisors suggested we evacuate immediately. I visited Colonel McGowan at US military headquarters. He and other advisers said that if VC held any part of the city, the Americans would probably have to use bombs to get them out.

I barely had time to tell Mai about Paris before our discussion turned to the AFSC team's current dilemma—leave Quảng Ngãi or be bombed by our own country? Mai suggested I write a letter to her mysterious NLF contact, "Uncle Nam." I described meeting with the Provisional Revolutionary Government and North Vietnamese official delegations in Paris, repeated the message that AFSC came to Vietnam to treat civilians on both sides of the conflict, and reminded him that we wished to stay, no matter what government was in power, to continue our work.

This time, Mai asked me to include a map with the letter, indicating the location of the Rehabilitation Center and AFSC house. It was easy to draw the location of the Center since the building was within the walls of the local hospital. It was difficult, however, to mark the location of the AFSC house relative to other landmarks such as the marketplace and airport. I tried to draw buildings with the right proportions and an accurate distance from each other. Mai sent the letter off to the mountains, this time "by courier," sewn into the hem of the message bearer's pant leg. Mai said it was essential to know where the AFSC house was located "when the NLF takes over the city." She said this with assurance. What did she know? The fighting had been increasing these past few weeks.

In the following months, as the Americans started to withdraw, fighting was left to the South Vietnamese ARVN soldiers. Many were afraid of the men and women in the NLF, who had proven to be tough, committed fighters. They might all be Vietnamese, but the NLF had the advantage of fighting for a cause they believed in, while most ARVN were drafted. Being aligned with the Americans had brought them certain advantages—money, supplies they could steal and sell on the black market, a vehicle, and means of collecting bribes. Ironically, though, the US military attacked this region ferociously, including the creation of free fire zones over the Batangan Peninsula, the peninsula remained an NLF stronghold, with layers of underground tunnels, some large enough to accommodate a water buffalo.

One day, Mai confirmed "Uncle Nam" had received the letter and map.[23] Although I didn't know Uncle Nam's rank or position at that time, a Mennonite friend met him after liberation and learned he was the First Communist Party Secretary of Quảng Ngãi Province. I had been communicating with the highest-ranking NLF official in our area.

---

23 When "Uncle Nam" answered my letter, it was short and optimistic. He mentioned it wouldn't be too long until the liberation of Quảng Ngãi and added an explicit instruction: "When the NLF sends AFSC a specific number, they should paint it in big letters on a large piece of fabric or a board to hang on the fence of the Quaker house." He didn't say how or when we would receive the mystery number but led us to believe it would spare the residence from attacks, at least from the NLF. Indeed, in March 1975, when the NLF/PRG took over Quảng Ngãi, remaining staff were notified to hang a number on the gate to identify the house.

CHAPTER 5

Torture and Tiger Cages
Prisons in Quảng Ngãi Province

From the beginning of its humanitarian programs in Vietnam and in alignment with the Quaker belief that there is "light in everyone," AFSC was able to establish a medical visitation program inside the prison of Quảng Ngãi. One AFSC doctor, Marge Nelson, testified before Congress that in 1970, she had treated prisoners in the Quảng Ngãi prison who had been tortured and documented cases. No concrete action was taken by the US government, which provided funds for the prison and its personnel.

Starting in 1970, there was a huge increase in random sweeps and the number of people detained. There was not enough room in the local prison; instead, barracks along the main road held people, arrested for their political beliefs, not for any crimes committed.

Two years before the Paris Peace Accords were signed, US troops started to disengage from direct fighting. The United States attempted to transfer most military operations to ARVN forces as the morale of US troops declined, military funding cuts began, and American and ARVN forces became less confident about winning. Meanwhile, South Vietnamese males of fighting age were either drafted or required to carry papers explaining why they were exempt. ARVN soldiers and South Vietnamese military police stepped up, detaining and questioning civilians. They were political prisoners, even though President Thieu, during a visit to the Vatican in April 1973, stated, "There are no political prisoners in South Vietnam.

There are only common law criminals and Communist criminals."[24]

Women were the most vulnerable to suspicion. Randomly, they were rounded up by military police and questioned about their activities, if they had any contact with the NLF, and what they might know. They were asked whether they had brothers, fathers, or husbands sympathetic to the NLF or if they had acted on behalf of the NLF themselves. Anyone with relatives who had gone north in 1954, when Vietnam was temporarily divided, were questioned. Were they or their relatives assisting the NLF? ARVN forces arrested women traveling in, or near, a contested area, even if they had lived there all their lives. The US government issued a contract to Honeywell, an American corporation, to photograph every South Vietnamese family and provide them with a plastic identification card. The program was poorly implemented, and errors were common. There was a good chance not everyone in the family was available the day pictures were taken. Most Vietnamese had never been photographed before and were unsure of the government's reasons. Some were physically forced to have their photos taken.

Interrogation Compound holding political prisoners, located on main street of Quang Ngai, Vietnam

---

24 Kennedy, Ted, *Congressional Record*, Monday, June 4, 1973.

In Quảng Ngãi, there was a block-long complex of multiple rows of simple structures with concertina wire-topped fences around them. At one end was a building for interrogating political prisoners. Looking at the interrogation compound, in full view on the main street, I saw the hands of prisoners stretching above the tarp wrapped around the fence, trying to signal a loved one or relative. The scene reminded me of photos of World War II concentration camp prisoners reaching for the sky above a barbed wire fence. A canvas tent anchored one corner of the compound where relatives stood in the scorching heat to ask the whereabouts of a family member or friend. Occasionally, the guards allowed families to leave supplies for the prisoners, especially if a hefty bribe was included.

Until after the visit in 1972 by the staff of US Senator Ted Kennedy, who chaired the Senate Judiciary Committee, we thought the only location where political prisoners were held was in this block-long row of barracks called the interrogation compound. However, before this congressional fact-finding group arrived, the Vietnamese authorities were altering the landscape, starting with the hospital grounds, which were spiffed up, raked, and tidied. When I joined staffers on their tour, I noticed a small building, previously a storage building, was now occupied. I couldn't immediately determine why there were people in this building; I wanted to keep pace with the staffers. As soon as the Senate delegation left, I made inquiries.

We discovered that US/South Vietnamese authorities had removed select prisoners from the interrogation compound to the shed before the official US government representatives had arrived, with the intention of hiding those critically injured during torture—just in case the senator's staff asked to tour the compound. After this incident, a pattern developed. American CIA or South Vietnamese-trained specialists at the compound, fearful a prisoner might die from torture, transferred the prisoner to the "secret" ward on hospital grounds. Officials thought it better for a prisoner to die there, where it might be attributed to disease, than at the interrogation compound, which might raise questions.

I accompanied the AFSC doctor on regular visits to the small building, which we Quakers called the Political Prison Ward, to serve as an interpreter.[25] The compact building held about fourteen beds. Two prisoners were chained to each bed using "made in America" Smith & Wesson handcuffs.

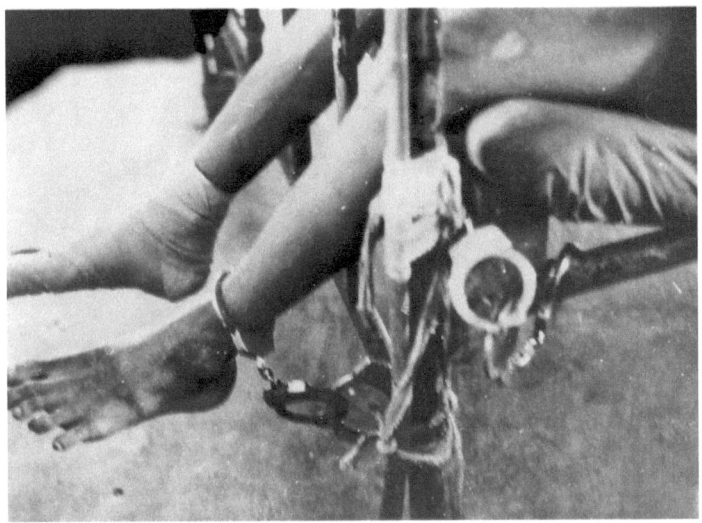

Male political prisoner handcuffed to bed with American manufactured Smith & Wesson handcuffs

Among them was a twelve-year-old boy, captured for carrying two vials of medicine in a contested area. He had been beaten to reveal the delivery location. Yet, he insisted the medicine wasn't intended for the NLF but for his ailing grandfather. The boy's father was a nurse at the hospital. Even having a father working for the South Vietnamese government didn't seem to matter. No one checked into the cause of the boy's arrest; there were no formal interrogations and never any trials. A sixty-seven-year-old woman, picked up near an area thought to be held by the NLF, lay on a piece of cardboard, with a hole cut in it so

---

25   AFSC staff serving in Vietnam usually spent two months in language study. Since most doctors who came to Vietnam stayed for only a few months at a time, they did not take language training and depended on other AFSC staff to translate for them.

she could defecate into a bowl under the bed. She had been paralyzed from injuries due to torture. Her head was shaved because no staff were available to help incapacitated prisoners wash their hair or clothes.

Twelve-year-old male political prisoner

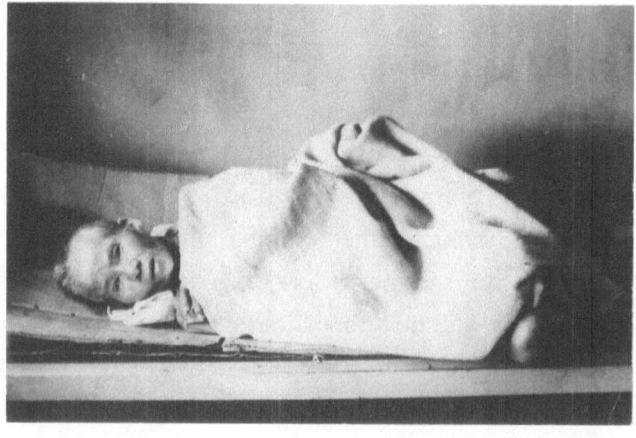

Sixty-seven-year-old woman paralyzed from being tortured

Vietnamese prisoners reported they were tortured by American or Vietnamese specialists in a room inside the interrogation compound. It was a common belief that the CIA was directly involved in training South Vietnamese military and police forces in torture methods. The CIA was established in a small, heavily fortified house in Quảng Ngãi, with lots of antennas on the roof. The men lived separately from the US military forces and emerged from their house in enclosed vehicles.

Political prisoner who suffered seizures after being tortured with electricity

Many women in the ward had seizures, foaming at the mouth from neurological damage. They described the ways they were tortured or repeated what they might have cried out during their ordeal: "Stop. I'm dying!" They said the torture often started with electrical wires attached to their nipples or genitals. Their stomachs were filled with water and beaten until they vomited. They were forced to stand on a small box for hours. Although waterboarding was a term I had not heard at the time, the women described having their heads held under water for long periods. Sometimes they were tied to long boards, which were then tipped into buckets, their heads under water, until they felt they would explode.

Two journalists secretly accompanied me into the prison ward: Jacques Leslie, a war correspondent for the *Los Angeles Times*, and Martin Woollacott of Britain's *Guardian*. Leslie reported what they saw:

> The ward's twenty-four residents shared fourteen beds, two of which lacked a mattress. . . . Though tortured months or even years earlier, many of the women suffered residual seizures as often as several times a day. Suddenly a woman . . . began moaning, writhing, and furiously pounding her bed with her fists and legs. Though the women were all chained to their beds, the other patients quietly proceeded to use cloth strips to tie the woman down so she couldn't hurt herself. . . . Like a grenade lobbed into an ammo dump, the first seizure induced another one, and another and another. Martin and I stared dumbfoundedly as everyone . . . was soon either convulsing or caring for someone who was.
>
> We talked later to one of the ward's patients. . . . Eighteen years old, she had a gaze so deep I could see miles into her eyes. She fought for the Viet Cong—she said so. Two of her friends were killed, and she was wounded and captured. For twenty-three days, she was alternately beaten. . . . She said the beatings were so fierce, she didn't know pain anymore. "I was already dead."[26]

The regular guard seemed unconcerned with our visits. Perhaps he was sympathetic to the prisoners, as he often stepped away from the building to stroll around and smoke a cigarette when the AFSC physician and I made medical visits. Later I wondered if he was working undercover for the NLF. The women were particularly at ease with me. They knew what AFSC stood for, and they would pat a spot on their beds for me to sit. I asked questions and jotted notes. I carried my camera in a small blue canvas bag. The guard never asked

---

26   Leslie, Jacques, *The Mark*, Four Walls Eight Windows, New York/London, 1995, p. 167.

to look in it, and I took my camera back to the Quaker house to develop and print the film. I mailed some to the main AFSC office. They sat untouched until I returned a year later, when the topic of Vietnamese prisoners began to be of interest to the US Congress and general population.

It is hard for me to write about the torture even now, fifty years later, knowing that it continues and is still subsidized by the US. In 2003, I saw a photograph of a man with a black hood over his head. The prisoner's head had electrical wires attached to his extremities as he stood on a box inside Abu Ghraib Prison, with US military personnel laughing nearby. As much as I tried to alert Americans to the horrors, mistreatment, and humiliation of Vietnamese prisoners, torture by the US has continued at so-called "black sites," including Guantanamo. My efforts to document torture stories, photograph victims, testify before Congress, and speak publicly while sponsored by Amnesty International were to little avail.

On January 27, 1973, the Paris Peace Accords were signed, calling for the release of American and Vietnamese POWs. Some of the AFSC team and I went to the Quảng Ngãi airport to watch planes arrive with POWs aboard. They had been held outside of Quảng Ngãi, including at the infamous Con Son prison on an island off the coast of Vietnam. Two months later, AFSC received two prisoners for treatment at the Rehabilitation Center.

Both were paralyzed from the waist down after being confined in underground tiger cages, cells topped with metal bars over which the guard would walk. The cells were so small that prisoners couldn't stand upright, causing their leg muscles to atrophy. These former prisoners used small wooden "stools" to scoot around on the floor. A BBC film crew shot a dramatic documentary, *A Queston of Torture*, revealing, after their release, these prisoners skittering around like crabs. The crew also interviewed David and me. There was a loud bang during the filming, and I remember telling the film crew, "Don't worry. Outgoing—Americans firing a four-deuce mortar."

The POWs were handsome young men who impressed me with their resolve. Each wore a shirt sewn of different fabrics in a patchwork. They were made, they said, from remnants of shirts of other prisoners who died or were released. I asked them to tell me their stories. They had been imprisoned while I was in college, traveling and exploring opportunities. The interview with them sparked a sense of survivor's guilt and a deep awareness of my privileged state.

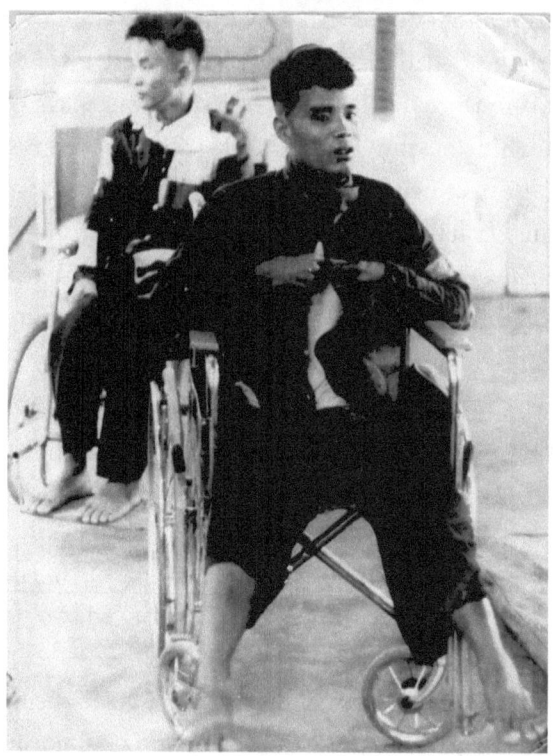

Two prisoners released from years spent in the Tiger Cages

CHAPTER 6

Visit to NLF Village as a Russian
& Special AFSC Vietnamese Staff

A simple Buddhist temple on our mountain, built in 1695 and tended by three monks, was a tiny oasis of peace—even though it overlooked the villages where the My Lai massacres occurred. On occasional Sundays, the AFSC team invited Vietnamese friends to play frisbee there, the rusty VW van groaning as it struggled up the steep incline of the red clay road. Mai didn't join us on these excursions, although we were good friends then. Perhaps she didn't come along because frisbee was a difficult physical activity for her. Or maybe she wasn't interested in being seen outside the Rehab Center with Americans. Her preferred places were the door of the Rehab Center or her bedroom. So, I was surprised when, not long after I sent the letter to "Uncle Nam," Mai suggested that she, David, and I take a Sunday trip.

The ostensible purpose was to take a young girl, Hang, with one below-the-knee (BK) amputation from stepping on a mine, back to her village. The village was in the direction of the mountains, west of the airport, off the main paved Route 1 that stretched the length of Vietnam, north to south. Mai suggested a six-year-old was too young to travel alone. The child's family didn't know if Hang was dead or alive since there was no communication after she was taken to the hospital. The family, as far as I knew, was not aware we were bringing her home.

As Hang recovered, Mai arranged for an eleven-year-old girl to come after school to help her. It wasn't unusual to find an older child taking care of a younger sibling or a young child caring for a parent for months at a time. One task was bringing food to patients from a large vessel rolled out daily onto the hospital grounds. The caregiver would bring a small container and scoop some food—usually watery broth with vegetables—from the big pot and carry it to their charge.

The trip to the mountains was quiet. Mai was usually exuberant but seemed subdued and almost anxious. She sat in the back seat, leaning forward as if to study the landscape for landmarks. Sometimes Mai and Hang spoke to each other in hushed voices. The day before, Mai surprised me, saying she would introduce us as Russians when we arrived. This was the first time Mai had ever made such a suggestion. She could quote the Quaker spiel as well as anyone on our team. What was wrong with us representing a US humanitarian organization, helping both sides of the conflict? Did Mai think the reputation of AFSC's work had not reached this far? It didn't make sense, but sometimes Mai didn't explain her reasons. I later understood, as Russians, we were less likely to be detained or shot by the NLF.

It was a pleasant visit to the village. Like most villages, older women and children made up the majority of the population. Children stared at us with curiosity but didn't clamber after us calling, "*Anh My, Ba My*" ("Mr. America, Mrs. America"). That was a frequent taunt in South Vietnam- and US military-controlled regions, where we became pied pipers with hordes of kids following us down dirt lanes. In those places, when we went into a house with walls of woven bamboo, or sticks and wattle, the children pushed to look through a window or doorway with such force that I was afraid the house might collapse. Such a crush happened when AFSC physician John Talmadge, Bich, and I administered vaccines during an outbreak of bubonic plague. John described it like this:

> Vietnam is a curious place. I don't mean curious like weird. I mean like what-the-hell-is-going-on-and-so-let's-go-look-at-it. . . . I saw a case of suspected bubonic plague—bubonic, the kind you read about in the Bible—in a small

hut on an island off the coast of Vietnam, and nearly every person in the village tried to get into that hut with me. Now imagine being so curious that you would join a mob of fifty to a hundred people to share bubonic plague, just to see what is going on.[27]

In situations like this, an elder usually shooed the children away and brought order. I had become accustomed to attracting clusters of children, yet in Hang's village, children stared but didn't crowd us. They had serious expressions but none of the unfriendly glares—or taunts.

As soon as Mai introduced us to Elder Sister Chuc, whose name meant chrysanthemum, we were invited into a one-room dwelling, tucked into a grove of trees, to have tea. The roof was thatched, and the sides were made of woven banana leaves. It occurred to me that it might be difficult to spot from the air. Two other women, Xuan (Spring) and Thu (Autumn), joined us.

Almost instantly, Hang's parents arrived. There was affection but no tears or outward emotional expression, yet the faces of the father, mother, and child radiated relief and joy. The father was thin but muscular and strong. Hang's mother ran her hands through her daughter's hair, soothing and caressing. They didn't seem concerned with her prosthesis, which was covered by the leg of her trousers. There is an honest manner in the way Vietnamese people look at another person's body. As Americans, we often "sneak a peek" at a person with special needs, being careful not to stare. In Vietnam, I found that people looked openly as they processed what they saw—an artificial leg. For example, they might pepper Mai with questions such as "Is the leg made of wood? How does the leg bend? What holds the leg on?" Hang's parents made brief conversation and thanked us for the prosthesis. Then the little girl and her parents disappeared.

We were in "liberated" territories—in other words, an NLF-controlled village. Mai, David, and I chatted with Chuc and

---

27   Letter from John Talmadge to AFSC headquarters, July 8, 1972.

two other women. They were dressed in the typical *ao* and *quams* (blouse and black pants) of farming people. Their demeanor was more confident than I was accustomed to. Often, Vietnamese who worked in areas controlled by the US and South Vietnamese military were outwardly deferential, almost subservient to authority, but in this zone, far from foreign influence, these women possessed a manner that demanded respect.

Our conversation started with the usual questions Vietnamese were apt to ask: "Are you married? Do you have children? How old are you? Are your parents alive? How many siblings are there in your family? Do you like Vietnam?" Most conversations in South Vietnam-controlled areas avoided politics, but these women eagerly quizzed us about what we thought of the US government. Then they launched into a speech about the long struggle of the Vietnamese against their many oppressors to gain independence. Thu leaned over to me, saying in Vietnamese, "The revolution is *vui*." In conversation, when I used the term *vui*, I referred to something fun, but in this case, I believe she was trying to tell me the revolution was "rewarding."

Village hospitality included the ubiquitous tea and peanuts. Often, we would be offered store-bought or homemade sweets, but food must have been scarce since, this time, it was limited to peanuts. Xuan led David and me on a short walk to examine village buildings, one of which served as a school. As we got closer, I saw single-person shelters dug into the ground, some with metal tops and others with thick covers of woven fibers. I had never seen these before. In the city, bunkers were large, concrete structures, holding several people. These small shelters were holes in the ground, designed for school children to pop into during an attack, large enough for one or two children. Most had wooden covers, with natural materials attached as camouflage. Obviously, this region must be receiving military fire from planes or helicopters. There were probably fewer than ten students in the school.

The village was small. We rejoined Mai, Chrysanthemum, and Thu, and before engaging in the usual polite thank-yous and goodbyes, a man abruptly appeared. He was introduced as Uncle Nam, meaning "number five," a name given to the fifth-born child in a family. I doubted it was his real name, and I did not assume he was the person I had exchanged letters with. Uncle Nam had an unassuming yet dignified manner. We discussed the war, and Uncle Nam repeated a Vietnamese phrase often: "It is not the American people who are our enemies, only the American government." He knew there were Americans who actively opposed the war. David and I talked about the role of the American Friends Service Committee in organizing and participating in demonstrations against the war. We said, just before coming to Vietnam, we engaged in antiwar activity and marches to build public pressure. It was a challenging conversation. Mai offered a word or two when my Vietnamese faltered. I was proud of our coordination in front of someone who was likely a high-ranking NLF official. No one offered information about Uncle Nam, and I was surprised when Mai suggested we pose for a picture, which she took with my camera. Uncle Nam wished us well, and we got into the van, minus Hang, to return to Quảng Ngãi.

Anh Nam with Jane and David Barton

The ride back was almost silent, highly unusual for Mai. I wanted to say, "What the hell was all that? Where did you take us? Who was that man who mysteriously appeared as we were leaving?" I was baffled and a bit angry for not being better informed. Each of us was processing the trip in our minds. It was beastly hot as we drove back to the AFSC house.

I'd like to say that Mai eventually gave me an explanation. But she didn't. Did we go to a village near Mai's *que* (ancestral home)? Were any of her family members present? What were Mai's ties to the village? Then there was posing as Russians. My suspicion was that Mai wanted to make her physical presence known—to show someone who could send word to family and friends that she was alive. Maybe the Russian connection was a cover in case someone who couldn't be trusted, or was later captured, had to explain the presence of two Westerners that day.

An enigmatic trip into liberated territories was a test of Mai's trust in me. Afterward, she seemed more open about her political sympathies, but she didn't divulge details about her life, even her true name. "Mai" was undoubtedly a nom de guerre; revealing her real name could risk her life.

I was curious to know more about her on a personal level. Instead, Mai told me about life, in general terms, in the liberated areas. She explained how the NLF professed a doctrine of equality between the sexes and encouraged the use of the more familiar terms "brother" and "sister" in place of the traditional hierarchy of courtesy titles. The ranking system of how to address Vietnamese individuals was challenging. There were numerous honorifics. If a woman was older, I might refer to her as *chi*, older sister. But if she was older and married, I would call her *ba*. A younger woman, I could call *em*, but if I used the term with someone of equal rank and standing to me, it would be insulting. The NLF system appealed to me since it aligned with the Quaker concept that all people are equal.

Mai related tales of women who rose to be leaders and participated in what American feminists called "consciousness-raising sessions." Mai said the NLF included these sessions in its educational training of male and, especially, female cadres. She knew about the "Long-Haired Army," the all-female unit I read about in contemporary history articles. She also described how International Women's Day was celebrated by both the NLF and the Communist Party. For many years after the war ended, Mai sent me International Women's Day greetings. In the US, I had few reminders of International Women's Day—until Mai's cards arrived.

Kiem

Kiem, one of Mai's closest friends, also shared tales of life in liberated areas. Kiem arrived at the Rehabilitation Center after being severely injured by US soldiers. She was less guarded than Mai and loved having an audience. Kiem was a dancer in a cultural troupe, traveling throughout southern Vietnam, entertaining soldiers in a style diametrically different from United Service Organization (USO) shows that featured sexy actresses and raunchy humor to boost morale.

These Vietnamese cultural programs were sweet and nostalgic. Musicians played sentimental songs on traditional Vietnamese instruments. Actors dramatized mothers and lovers longing for their soldiers' return. Recitation of poetry was a major feature, and a favorite song played on the flute was guaranteed to bring tears. Performances were held in jungles and the mountains. Kiem believed they improved the morale of soldiers and reminded them they were part of a united effort to free their country from an aggressive foreign power. Kiem described cultural troupes as living symbols of the Vietnamese commitment to national unity. She insisted she was not merely a performer of traditional dances but part of a team who faced terrible adversity as they traveled to perform and arouse nationalist pride.

Kiem's scars and pockets of missing flesh affirmed this. Before one troupe performance, a makeshift structure had been erected with a canopy of tree leaves for camouflage. But despite this careful planning, a surveillance plane must have located their activity. Helicopters airlifted American troops into the NLF location. Kiem had hidden in an underground tunnel big enough to hold eight people. She was the first one pulled out by American soldiers.

Waving her arms, Kiem described how a soldier took his machine gun and—in an instantaneous blaze—raked bullets across her in one direction, then turned the gun and shot her from the other direction. She was shot through both arms; her stomach and one leg were torn to pieces. In the My Lai massacre investigation, a soldier reported cutting a woman in two with bullets from his machine gun. I hadn't realized the gun was that powerful. Kiem was fortunate to be alive. Ironically, American military forces saved her by airlifting her to the hospital in Quảng Ngãi. Kiem remembers a Vietnamese doctor providing triage treatment and then being left on a stretcher on the unsanitary floor of the hallway. Kiem, like Mai years before, had no family to bring her food or bribe nurses for medicine.

Two days after waking up in the hospital, Kiem remembers the AFSC orthopedic surgeon, Chuck Henkel, passing along the hospital corridor and stopping at her stretcher. He knelt, lifted one of her arms, and sniffed it. Kiem thought this was bizarre behavior. She didn't know he was smelling for gangrene. If Chuck had detected it, he might have passed over her to another patient he was more likely to save. Instead, he had Kiem moved to the AFSC hostel. Chuck eventually performed seven operations on her leg, which was intact but had areas with flesh missing. The limb was too mangled to perform naturally, but Chuck was determined to save it so it could be fitted with a brace.

The skilled Rehab Center staff designed a brace with a canvas "hammock" in which Kiem's leg rested. She used her hip muscles to swing the brace forward. The leg played no part in helping her walk, but it was her own and not a prosthetic device. When her leg was covered with a pant leg, it wasn't possible to tell she was injured until she started to walk. Eventually, her stomach, arms, and other leg healed, and the holes in her body were sealed by skin grafts and stitches. She let me feel the pieces of shrapnel pushing their way out of her body and delighted in knowing the metal reminders of her near-death experience were leaving.

None of these injuries diminished Kiem's beauty. She had a dimple and a teasing sense of humor. She described life with the cultural troupe as a joyful time. She and other talented members of the company always looked forward to their next presentation. Her work was appreciated, and she loved being part of the movement to bring freedom to her country. I'm not sure how Kiem came to work as a cook in the AFSC house or to share Mai's bedroom, but soon she was part of the AFSC family.

Kiem so worshiped Chuck that I was surprised when I once heard her criticize him. She had seen Chuck and his wife coming out of the Protestant church in town. Kiem regarded followers of Protestant or Catholic churches as supporters of foreign domination. She resented foreign intervention on all levels, including the introduction of Western religions. I understood why the doctor and his wife, Midwestern and traditionally religious, might enjoy going to church. At the same time, I empathized with Kiem. Foreign churches seduced people to join. The Catholic Church converted people when priests arrived during the French occupation. Now a wave of Protestant churches entered Vietnam. Protestant converts, for example, received better access to medicine and other privileges. The same was true for Vietnamese Catholics, thanks to funds sent to support missionary work in Vietnam.

Transitions at the Rehabilitation Center

By mid-1973, the Rehab Center was managed and operated mainly by our Vietnamese staff. Chuck had trained his assistant, Bich, to perform excellent, delicate skin graphs and amputations, and an extraordinary man, Quy, led the prosthetic work. Western staff continued their role of witnessing and writing about the war and provided a critical safety umbrella for Vietnamese staff, like Mai, lessening the likelihood they would be arrested. Additionally, AFSC provided salaries for workers and facilitated funds arriving in Vietnam without graft or corruption.

Quy was a silent wild card. His small, down-turned mouth gave him a serious demeanor. Quy never questioned what he was taught—he just soaked it all up. When he became director of the Center, he launched a quiet revolution. He replaced the imported, expensive knee bolts used for above-knee prostheses with locally made bolts. First, he searched for the maker of an aluminum rice-cooking pot belonging to his mother. Through word of mouth, Quy found the metalworker who said he could make bolts at a low price because only labor was involved. The aluminum was free—cast off from American flares and plane parts. But if Quy wanted brass knee bolts, the metalworker could also supply those. Children and adult refugees regularly collected brass artillery shells from around firebases, but there wasn't as much available as aluminum, and brass bolts would be a bit more expensive.

Quy

In one of my reports back to the AFSC headquarters, dated June 26, 1972, I quote Quy gleefully remarking on the low price: "The aluminum knee bolt will cost 300 piasters; brass, 500 piasters. The comparison price is 3,800 for a knee bolt purchased in Hong Kong. Plus, there is the advantage of removing the preordering wait time of 3-6 months and the cost of shipping and getting through Vietnamese customs without being taxed."[28]

Quy's next quest was to find a native plant used to dye monks' robes brown during the French occupation. On one Sunday trip to Buddha Mountain, Quy came. He disappeared and suddenly reemerged from the bushes, carrying plants pulled up by the roots, dirt falling. Although Quy held his emotions in check, he was ecstatic. Back at the Center, he boiled the roots and dyed the cotton covering used for prosthetics a tan color, matching the skin tone of patients. Quy informed us AFSC could stop ordering the pink dye imported from Hong Kong.

Why hadn't the Western staff noticed pink was inappropriate? The two British prosthetists trained their Vietnamese students to make a realistic-looking leg, but neither Quy nor the student trainees mentioned skin tone. They also trained students to make a foot for walking on flat surfaces, like sidewalks. But innovative Quy, noting there were no cement or brick sidewalks in all of Quảng Ngãi Province, focused on creating a leg to be used while working—a leg for fishermen and one for either men or women to use in the rice fields.

Quy then tackled the issue of hook-arms, the AFSC standard for patients who had lost an arm, and I was fascinated with how he approached this. I had noticed, in follow-up visits, many former single-arm patients did not use their hook-arm consistently. Most depended on their good arm. They considered the hook unattractive and minimally useful.

One day, after studying a display of black-market plastic dolls in the marketplace, Quy decided to replicate their hands, a semi-closed

---

28 Report by Jane Barton to AFSC headquarters, June 26, 1972.

position with the fingers and thumb curved. After multiple trials, Quy found the most successful model to be a hand with four fingers connected and touching the thumb. Patients used it for tasks like picking up a drinking glass or holding the bamboo balancing pole Vietnamese use to transport everything from baskets of vegetables to children. With the prosthetic hand holding the pole, the other arm could pump the elbow, creating the rocking motion required to carry heavy loads.

But the favorite trick of patients who had lost their right arm was to wrap the artificial hand around the grip of their Honda motorbikes and cross over with their "good" left hand to turn the gear control. Maybe it didn't jibe with my high school driving instructor who taught us to "keep both hands on the wheel" for safety at all times, but Quy's artificial hands enabled a one-armed patient to drive again.

AFSC might have brought the expertise to Vietnam, but the success of the prosthetic department was due to the ingenuity, dedication, and selflessness of Quy. As soon as he was in charge, he made changes that must have percolated in his mind during his training. Patience and timing are Vietnamese virtues.

CHAPTER 7

Journalists Visit the Liberated Zone

I listened carefully and began to gather hints that Mai knew more about the movement to free her country from foreign domination than the average Vietnamese person in Quảng Ngãi. One day, for example, Mai mentioned Cuba, which surprised me. Aside from a select few educated Vietnamese, most of the population of Quảng Ngãi would be unaware of this small country. Since Cuba supported the liberation movement in Vietnam and Mai spoke positively about Cuba, it seemed that Mai had an educated background about the NLF. Another clue was the severity of Mai's injuries. Although civilians were injured every day, in all types of locations, Mai's injuries suggested she had been in or near a battle and therefore may have been living in a liberated area and confronted US or ARVN troops.

Frances FitzGerald

Mai knew about the antiwar movement in the US—and that AFSC was part of it—but I found out she understood much more about the Western press, its activities, and its role than I had realized. Journalist Frances FitzGerald and another reporter, Dan Southerland, visited the AFSC house the first week of April 1973. Frances was on assignment for *The New Yorker* to write a series about life in NLF territories. Dan was a reporter for the *Christian Science Monitor*. They had chosen to come to Quảng Ngãi and asked if I could arrange to get them into a liberated, NLF-controlled area of the province. This was a question for Mai.

Mai's eyes danced at the opportunity to help. "Well, of course, I can assist Frances FitzGerald. She wrote *Fire in the Lake*, one of the most important historical studies about Vietnam. It won a Pulitzer Prize."

Oh my, was I taken by surprise! Many Americans were unaware of the book or award. I begged Mai to reveal how she knew this. She responded with indignation, "Absolutely, I know of Frances FitzGerald. I listen to BBC radio and heard a review of *Fire in the Lake*." I grinned. Mai was always surprising me.

Frances was no ordinary person. I chuckled to think I would be bridging the social divide between the two women. I knew Frances's family background included a governor, the founder of the prestigious Groton School, and a civil rights activist.[29] Francis and Dan made their request on a Saturday, and I assumed it would be days before Mai could negotiate the trip. But Mai quickly made secret arrangements for them to enter NLF-controlled areas near the city. It was dangerous to go into the buffer zones where the two governments overlapped. ARVN could arrest or shoot anyone in these areas, even foreigners. And there were the mines. Mai needed to map out a safe route and procure a guide. The safety of the journalists had to be ensured. It posed a risk for her too if the journalists were caught by ARVN or American soldiers. She could be tortured until she identified her sources.

Mai told Frances and Dan to be ready to leave at eight a.m. No one dared travel too early since mines at crossings and bridges might not have been deactivated. *Wow, tomorrow*, I thought, surprised she could facilitate arrangements so quickly. Mai informed me where to drop off Frances and Dan the next day.

We headed out in the miniature Japanese truck with its cabin for

---

29 Frances's mother, Marietta Tree, was an amazing woman who was part of a coterie of the wealthiest and most influential people in America. Some were friends. Others, including the director John Huston and presidential candidate Adlai Stevenson, were her lovers. Marietta was appointed to the UN Commission on Human Rights, an elevated honor for a woman in the 1960s. Penelope Tree, Frances's half-sister, became a famous model and a muse of the equally famous photographer Richard Avedon.

two—Frances and me—with Dan sitting in the open back flatbed. We drove over the Tra Khuc River, past Buddha Mountain, and down another dirt road near the villages where the two My Lai massacres occurred. We passed the ditch where the bodies had lain four years prior and headed toward the Batangan Peninsula.

The landscape became bare. It was extremely quiet. This was once a lush region where a centuries-old dike system held back seawater from the brackish rice paddies. A year before, I traveled to this location with an employee who wanted to check on his family and see if the ancestral tombs had been bombed. The tombs were gone, but we found his mother living in a makeshift shack. Her house had been destroyed. She served us dried yam and sweet potato, apologizing that she had no rice. No vegetables. No coffee. Not even a banana. Any time I had been to this area, I had always arranged to send a warning ahead that AFSC staff were en route. Mai must have sent word this time.

It seemed odd to drop off journalists in such a deserted place. Mai had instructed me to watch for a certain bombed-out structure, missing its roof and side walls, and soon after that, a young boy in a gray *ao* (traditional-style Vietnamese shirt). As a signal, a vertical bundle of bamboo would be tied near the rear tire of his bicycle.

Boy who lead journalists FitzGerald and Southerland into NLF territory

I spotted him. His back was to me, and his *non* (conical hat) was thrown back, attached by a thin ribbon around his neck, forming a halo behind his head. The shirt and bamboo matched Mai's description. I slowed the truck. The boy raised his hand. With no words exchanged, Frances and Dan hopped out. Each had a small backpack with writing materials and some water.

This moment was critical. They had to get across a rice field and into the dense vegetation beyond, and I needed to get out of the area fast. By the time I looked down the road for a place to turn around, the scout and journalists had disappeared.

It was a few months before we saw anything Dan or Frances had written. Someone sent us a copy of Frances's story in *The New Yorker*. Here is an excerpt:

> In Quảng Ngãi, the transition could be made by walking across a road. On one side of the road where the ARVN troops patrolled, the people watched American television and listened to anti-Communist lectures from the Saigon officials. On the other side, in full view of the American-built airport, North Vietnamese troops stood watch behind a hedge. There the people spoke of liberation, imperialism and revolution.[30]

Trouble

In some ways, Frances FitzGerald's visit marked the beginning of the end of my time in Vietnam.

Our AFSC location usually had little contact with the South Vietnamese government, military, or civilian officials. But the day after Frances and Dan went into NLF-controlled territories, the top US State Department official in the region, Frederick Z. Brown, drove from Danang to Quảng Ngãi to pay us a special visit. Brown knew, of course, that Frances and Dan had stayed at the AFSC house. It was an awkward conversation. We would not lie to a State Department

---

30 Fitzgerald, Frances, *The New Yorker*, July 1, 1972, p. 10.

official, but we didn't want to endanger the journalists by identifying the area they had entered. I said I had given them a scenic tour of the town—one major intersection and no traffic lights is an indication of the size of downtown Quảng Ngãi—and they had asked to get out of the truck to explore on their own.

I told Brown I couldn't reveal where Frances and Dan had asked to get out of the truck because I didn't want the US or ARVN hunting them, an action that could cause both civilian and military injuries. Brown let us know AFSC was in Vietnam by the grace of the South Vietnamese government, and any attempt on our part to give journalists directions, access, or contacts with the enemy would bring repercussions—by the South Vietnamese government and ARVN military. Since the South Vietnamese government was nearly entirely funded by the US, we were aware that Brown would be making decisions about AFSC's future in Vietnam.

Brown seemed particularly agitated about Frances's disappearance. Was it because she was female? Or because of her famous family or her brilliant mind and skilled pen? Later, Frances told me the State Department was worried she'd been kidnapped for ransom from her wealthy family. That was strange since, throughout the war, the NLF had no pattern of ransom kidnapping.[31]

The visit by Fred Brown set off a series of actions. Within an hour, the province chief summoned me to his headquarters. David—and

---

31 Many years later, when I got to know Frances—by then, I called her "Frankie"—I admired her intelligent and unpretentious manner. Frankie and I would meet in Maine, where we both had summer houses or at political conferences. One winter in 2000, we met in New York City for dinner. She wore a calf-length down coat, perfect for a frigid evening. Frankie unzipped it but stopped before she got to the very bottom. Rather unfashionably, she simply stepped out of the coat in the upscale dining room and draped it on the back of her chair. I thought, *Anyone else would have thrown away or bought a new coat if the zipper was broken.* In fact, it was a strategic move, not a zipper malfunction. Frankie later explained to me that if she had opened the zipper all the way, she would have to bend over nearly to her toes to reconnect the zipper parts. By leaving a couple of inches zipped toward the bottom of the coat, Frankie could just step into the coat and pull up the zipper. Her brilliant solution confirmed to me that Frances and Mai were women of the same ilk.

I—thought it wise for him to accompany me so that, for the record, we could both hear, corroborate, and later evaluate what had transpired in the presence of the chief. However, the driver who came to pick me up made it clear that David was not to come along.

The contrast between those who supported the NLF and those living on US funds could be dramatic. South Vietnamese government officials and military were "owned" by the US. Some South Vietnamese soldiers might act with bravado, but most knew they represented a puppet government. In contrast, people I met with loyalties to the NLF had a quiet dignity and self-respect. Such differences were obvious even in how the two sides dressed. When I walked into the meeting with the province chief, he was wearing a starched green uniform, nicely pressed for such a hot July day. He had a slight potbelly, a bit unusual in our region (even among the corrupt), because rich foods and alcohol weren't easy for the South Vietnamese officials to acquire in Quảng Ngãi.

I had grown averse to two characteristics of many South Vietnamese officials loyal to the Thieu government. One was their penchant for large fake gold watches that hung loosely on the wrists of these diminutive Vietnamese men. The other was a long pinky fingernail. As an Asian art history major, I was familiar with portraits of Chinese Han empresses, like Cixi, with long fingernails or decorative nail guards. These indicated culture, breeding, and wealth attached to a class that didn't engage in manual labor and had servants to wash, dress, and feed them. It seemed that South Vietnamese officials adopted the long pinkie look to announce that they were (thanks to the Americans) above manual labor. The province chief probably used his pinkie to clean the wax in his ears.

So, there I was facing a man I didn't respect but who had certain power over me. The interrogation started in English. The province chief didn't question so much as accuse me of being a Communist sympathizer and using AFSC work to help the Communists. He threatened that I was undermining the efforts of people like him by suggesting Communists and sympathizers were good-intentioned people, helping poor peasants.

As he got angrier, he began to lose his English, and soon he was speaking Vietnamese. I responded in Vietnamese, which startled him. Few, if any, American military or government officials he encountered spoke Vietnamese or knew anything about his culture. He paused and smoked a cigarette. I was uncomfortable. I sensed he was finding me more dangerous now and suspecting the rest of the AFSC team spoke his language too. If I could talk to him in Vietnamese, I might be able to talk to Communists. He remained silent until he finished his cigarette. Then he dismissed me with a threat: "You will pay for this act against the government of the Republic of South Vietnam."

About three weeks after Frances and Dan came to Quảng Ngãi, Fred Brown stopped by again. He confirmed the journalists had returned to South Vietnamese territory, unharmed and in good health. I understood why the province chief and Fred Brown were troubled. The truth was escaping in print to the American public.

CHAPTER 8

Killer for Hire

In 1973, there were only three Westerners left on the AFSC team: David, me, and Rick Thompson, a young Quaker. David and I were waiting for replacements. Senior staff at AFSC Philadelphia headquarters suspected that the State Department was pressuring the South Vietnamese government to refuse visas for new directors, a doctor, and a physical therapist as a way to choke off the program. Besides facilitating journalist visits into liberated territories, AFSC's access to prisoners had become a problem. We received a letter from a newly appointed province chief, Colonel Loi, thanking us for our past work.

> . . . in this savage time of war, which the Communists have brought upon us . . . we admire your concern for serving the people of Vietnam *regardless of their color, race, religion, or politics* [a phrase taken from the letter we had written to Colonel Loi], but those evil people who kill innocent people yesterday and today, who are treated by your organization, do not change their cruel attitude, and we cannot grant your request to return to work in the prison.[32]

AFSC visits to the provincial prison, where those considered criminals were held, were banned, as were visits to the prisoner ward

---

32   Letter from Colonel Loi to AFSC team in Quảng Ngãi, Vietnam, February 10, 1973.

on hospital grounds. Colonel Bowman, American advisor to the province chief, agreed to meet. Bowman declared he had done his own research and expressed displeasure over Marge Nelson's congressional testimony two years earlier. He commented that Dr. Nelson had criticized the US for their leading role in training and conducting the torture of prisoners, as well as financing these operations. Bowman declared he had followed up and checked all of Nelson's allegations and found none of them to be true.

After more requests to US and Vietnamese officials, AFSC was finally allowed to visit the hospital prison ward. When we returned, at least a third of the patients had been removed, among them the most critically sick. Those who remained had minor ailments and were not victims of torture. I was most concerned about two female prisoners who officials said were taken back to the compound for "further interrogation." One had a serious cardiac issue and a bullet lodged in her leg. The other was a hemiplegic with a fractured skull. Owing to torture, she was partially paralyzed and unable to walk. I wrote a letter to the province chief and head of the interrogation compound, which AFSC physician John Talmage signed, requesting their release because further confinement constituted a threat to their life and health.[33]

News reports were starting to come out about the treatment of prisoners in Vietnamese jails. An article by Sydney Schanberg appeared on the front page of the *New York Times* Sunday edition on August 13, 1972. A photograph, taken by a representative of the humanitarian organization who went with Dr. Talmage into the prison ward, accompanied the article.

Rick

Without a full American staff, the house felt empty. Rick wasn't much younger than me, but he seemed like a kid. His mother sent him peanut butter, and he rode his scooter at night—recklessly close

---

33 Talmage, John Mills, letters requesting release of two seriously ill prisoners: Pham thi Tho and Nguyen thi Lang, August 8, 1972.

to the curfew—to get a small baguette, a legacy from the French occupation of Vietnam. The bread usually had a few weevils, but they were cooked, and Rick took no notice as he made his bedtime peanut butter sandwiches.

Rick had made friends with employees at the Center and was now testing out friendships with other Vietnamese he met in town. Like all of us, Rick was navigating an unfamiliar culture. We were always the center of curiosity and had to be skeptical of strangers who approached us. Were they genuinely curious about us as American civilians, or were they after a favor? What was this person's true affiliation? Were they really who they said they were? Did they think we were rich Americans who could give them something? Were they spies?

The AFSC house had no hired guards or physical barriers to protect us, except for a gate like those of our neighbors. The staff shied away from inviting government or military people to the house. This was our way of staying neutral. We stuck to friendships with patients and neighbors. We gave their pigs and chickens food scraps and followed the Vietnamese example of never wasting anything. We welcomed acquaintances with no (known) government links.

Rick was a warm Midwesterner. He was feeling his way on how to understand the Vietnamese. I didn't want to be patronizing, giving my opinion of his new friends, but one guy made me uneasy. Lan was supposedly a former policeman. He wore a camouflage green shirt and pants to remind me of his past employment. Lan made himself too comfortable in Rick's room, touching his things, turning over books to look at their covers, and picking up family photos.

There was one time when Rick popped out of the kitchen, where he was visiting with Lan, and announced he was going for his *bun me* (bread) run. Rick assured us he would be right back. Once we were alone, Lan asked me, without the usual oblique Vietnamese approach, for a bribe. "I have some confidential information about you," he said. "If you give me fifty thousand piasters, I will tell you this private information."

During the three years I had been in Vietnam, I had yet to be asked for a bribe. Revulsion must have showed on my face, but before I could answer, the former policeman warned me, "Be careful. What I know is information that could keep you alive." I was flustered but said, "I am not accustomed to paying money to friends, or anyone else. This is not how AFSC operates." I declined to give anything to Lan, even though he repeated this a few times. Rick returned and got busy spreading peanut butter on bread and offered some to his friend. I couldn't help but laugh when Lan took a bite, then stopped chewing. He reached into his mouth, took out the lump of peanut butter and bread, and said, "It got stuck on the roof of my mouth. I couldn't swallow it."

I immediately headed for Mai's room to tell her about my encounter with Lan and get her read on the situation. A bribe for information about me? What could this be about? We sat on her bed holding hands. She'd taken her legs off and was relaxing before bed. We were puzzled over the bribe request. Mai told me she would check into the background of this former policeman.

I wasn't sure how Mai could get information about him—a government supporter—since I thought, perhaps naively, she wouldn't have contacts inside the police system. When I went to bed, Mai suggested I lock the shutters. They didn't have locks, so I bought some the next day.

The next morning, I stopped by Rick's room and asked if he could come by the office. I told Rick about Lan's bizarre request, and Rick seemed as stunned as I was. He admitted seeing his friend going into the Quảng Ngãi interrogation compound. I told Rick this wasn't a good sign and asked if he could quiz Lan for information without revealing the bribe incident.

The Secret

Mai had nothing to tell me the next day, or the next. She said she hadn't been able to pick up any information yet. "Yet" was the key word. Three days after the bribe attempt, Mai and I sat on her bed in the evening. Usually lighthearted, even in the worst of circumstances, Mai was serious. I put my hands on her arm and assured her it was safe to tell me what she had learned.

"What I tell you is something that might risk my contact. You know when there is a double agent, that person's security is of utmost importance, right?" she said. "I was able to gain some information, but I need to be very distant from the source so no one can trace it back to me. I will need a couple of days to find a way to get you the information through someone else."

I responded, "Mai, seriously, now that you know the information, you also know I could be in danger, correct? You must tell me. I won't be able to sleep."

I knew she was worried. "Jane, you must sleep in different rooms in the house for the next couple of days until we can talk. Don't walk openly on the road on the way to the Center. Never drive marked AFSC vehicles, and certainly don't go on a scooter. Absolutely do not go with Trung to do any social work visits in the countryside. Do your work inside. If employees need to talk to you, I will convey the message or have them talk to David. You have the locks on the shutters now, right? Go lock them and stay low."

I pleaded with Mai for more details, but I knew her stubbornness. Friendship is about trusting the other person absolutely. I was scared but needed to wait for Mai's instructions.

Another two days went by. I stayed inside. Since Rick, David, and I were the only Western AFSC staff left, my absence wasn't missed because the Center was being run by the capable Vietnamese team. I told David about my fears. Rick said, "Hey, you know that former policeman guy who was over the other night? He asked if he could come to the house tonight and talk to you. Not David, just you."

Would he ask for a bribe again? Paying would compromise my ethics and be hurtful to the AFSC program, but I wondered how I was going to get information without a payoff.

Early evening before curfew, Lan arrived on a new motor scooter, wearing sunglasses and the skintight colored shirts typical of the South Vietnamese guys we called "cowboys"—Vietnamese pretending to be cool, Western men. This time, Rick didn't offer bread and peanut butter. Lan and Rick came into the team living room, and we visited over hot tea. Rick was practicing his Vietnamese, and he asked the meaning of a lot of words. Finally, Lan turned to me.

"When I was here last time, I had some information, but the timing wasn't right," he said. "I came back tonight because I feel you need to know that your life might be in danger."

I thought, *I live in a war zone. Of course my life is in danger*. I asked what he meant.

"You made the province chief very, very angry when you took the journalists into the liberated side." (I noticed, with interest, that he used the word "liberated.") I was quiet, nodding for him to go on. "The Americans wrote stories that made the Communists sound like nice people, and the province chief has been criticized by his Vietnamese and American superiors. The American government officials are really mad too," Lan said. "The province chief is afraid he will be demoted or assigned to an even more dangerous area than Quảng Ngãi, if there is such a place. So, he came up with an idea to divert attention from himself. The province chief has offered money to anyone who can kill you, an innocent American woman who is supposed to be a humanitarian. The killing must appear to be done by the Communists. In this way, what the journalist wrote isn't true. The Communists are bad people."

Lan's words took the air out of me. I tried not to lose face by showing I was frightened. I took a deep breath and began to ask questions. Lan was not very responsive. He said he didn't have the answers; he was just telling me what he heard. Even the amount to be paid to the hitman was unclear. Some told him it was a million piasters; others said just a half million.

David entered the room at the end of the conversation, and he, too, was shocked. After Lan departed, I waited a while and then walked across the courtyards to Mai's room. Kiem was there too. I let Mai hug me for a minute. She wasn't one to tolerate timidity. I needed to demonstrate my inner strength.

Mai confirmed everything. "Yes, the information is true. The province chief wants you killed in such a way that it looks like the Communists would kill a woman and, particularly, one who is called a humanitarian and is helping injured people."

I asked Mai how she thought the killer or killers might try to pull it off. The NLF might assassinate corrupt government officials or traitors, but Mai said everyone knew they rarely killed an innocent Vietnamese civilian and certainly not an American humanitarian worker. She was convinced that the population in Quảng Ngãi wouldn't believe such a story, but then she had her prejudice. I was concerned with keeping myself alive.

"The people of Quảng Ngãi might not accept it, but I don't want it to happen in the first place," I said. "What do I do now?"

We discussed ways to limit my exposure. Mai suggested I sleep in a different bedroom, sometimes Rick's room, the guest room, or empty rooms waiting for replacement staff. Our conclusion was that, while the province chief would like me dead, there were no takers to do the job, as far as we knew. Nor were we aware of any plans to have it happen right away. David and I were due to leave in a few months. We had been scheduled to serve two years in Vietnam but were already approaching the end of our third. Maybe I would be able to leave before they murdered me.

CHAPTER 9

Departing Vietnam

Suspicious Illness

Looking back, this period is shrouded in mist. My health declined. I showed no specific symptoms—no aches, fever, or diarrhea, the most common of any illness—but my energy was draining. I was too sick to make the effort to travel to Saigon or Danang to visit a doctor. I'd stopped walking to the Rehab Center to avoid being a target for a hit man. The noise, dirt, congestion, and walking were daunting. I stayed at the Quaker house to write, read, or sleep.

Although months had passed since I learned of the province chief's plan to have me "bumped off," I was always looking over my shoulder. Once, I was hit by a motorbike but wasn't injured. Another night, two men climbed a porch roof to get into the AFSC house. A noise scared them away. I was spooked by shadowy figures in the courtyard late one night after the whole town was locked down under curfew. Days passed without any incidents or threats toward me. Perhaps the province chief had thought better of his scheme to kill a Quaker woman.

The South Vietnamese and US State Department, however, remained resolute in their refusal to grant visas for replacements for David and me. Perhaps they hoped AFSC would stop funding the Vietnamese staff. But this would not happen. AFSC was committed to providing operating costs for the Rehabilitation Center with Western staff, on site or not. While a US soldier's normal tour of duty was twelve months, AFSC staff were asked to serve two years.

David and I had been in Vietnam well over two years, and I was ill, tired, and jumpy.

My life was in danger. My body seemed to be wasting away.[34] I was living in a war zone, fighting was increasing, and there was a reward to have me killed. Yet nothing was as devastating as discovering my husband's betrayal. Even before I was sleeping in different rooms as a safety precaution, I noticed David was not always in bed. I convinced myself he had gone to the bathroom or was looking for a midnight snack. I usually fell asleep before he came back.

Discovery

The moment of discovery came one day, midmorning, when I happened to walk by the bomb shelter inside the house. It was usually vacant, especially during the day, and I had no reason to go inside. But I had an ominous feeling. I stuck my head into the bunker. Kiem and David were embracing. My reaction was visceral: my head swam, knees weakened, and heart exploded. I felt like my skin was being ripped off.

The shock and pain of this deception remained imprinted in my mind for decades. It was a dual violation. My husband was involved in a romantic—and likely physical—relationship with Kiem. And Kiem was Mai's best friend, a dear friend of mine. Despite her injuries and leg in a brace, it was possible to be intimate with David. Kiem was beautiful, charming. I'd noticed her adoration of him, although she wasn't the only Vietnamese woman to enjoy his teasing.

That moment was the finale of my time in Vietnam. The handsome man, the injured female warrior, and the loyal wife. If I had owned a sword, I would have struck down the lovers like a heroic figure from Vietnamese literature. Kiem and David knew I'd seen them. Our eyes met. From that moment, I rarely spoke to

---

34 I was suffering from a fatal, cyclical parasite that wasn't diagnosed until 1976 by a British tropical disease specialist doing research in the US. He acquired a trial medicine that was not approved in the US. The side effects were serious. I happened to be pregnant, and the doctors insisted I have an abortion before giving me the medicine.

either of them. I wanted to slip away, to leave Vietnam. David never offered an explanation, and I never asked. I was too sick at heart to confront him.

The relationship between David and Kiem put a strain on my friendship with Mai. How much did she know? Kiem and Mai shared a room, so when Kiem was missing in the middle of the night, did Mai have suspicions? Did she fear telling me?

Mai and I still visited and talked, but not like we used to. She said she was working on a project, and I suspected, correctly, that she was making a goodbye gift and needed time alone. Soon, Mai surprised me with yet another of her talents, an embroidered pillow cover. Vietnamese people don't use large Western-style sleeping pillows, but they sometimes place small, token pillows on their beds. It was a labor of love.

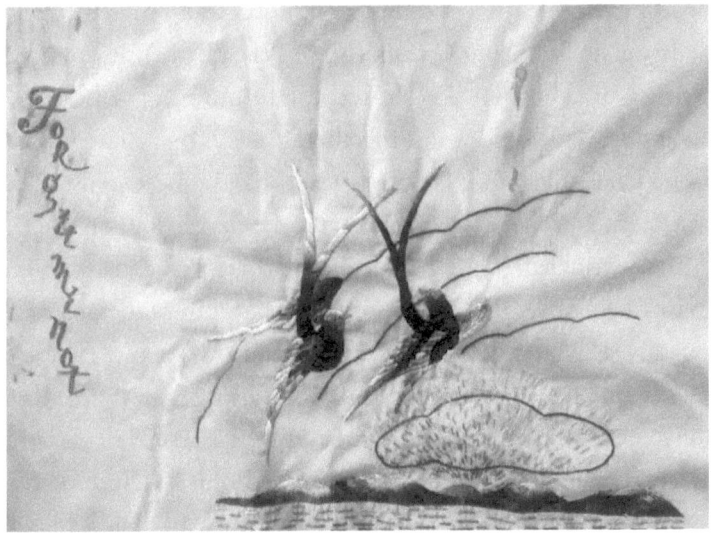

Pillow cover embroidered by Mai

In the center of the cover was a bouquet of delicate blue flowers with the words, "For get me not." I still chuckle when I see it. Mai had unknowingly made two words out of "forget." Her attempt in English was another Mai revelation. How did she know the name and shape of this flower, not native to Vietnam, and its symbolism of remembrance and loyalty?[35]

Leaving Quảng Ngãi

Another month passed. We heard, with relief, that two new directors, a doctor from Vermont and a physical therapist from Australia, would be on their way soon. It was time for David and me to leave.

Leaving Vietnam was wrenching. The staff at the Center was kind, and there were goodbye gifts and thank-yous. But being so sick in body and heart, I was relieved to escape the stress of the war. I lived in constant fear of the province chief. At the same time, I was cutting ties to an important period of my life—a time when I learned Vietnamese and came to know the country's history and culture, found myself sensitized to the challenges of people with disabilities, made a friend who had become a sister, and directed a successful program that was handed over to Vietnamese staff. There was an intensity that came from living on adrenaline. What did the future hold? Where would David and I live? Would we be together?

Once Mai told me, "David is really handsome because he has straight black hair like a Vietnamese and dark eyes. You, on the other hand, have wrinkled, white hair like an old woman and faded eyes." She wasn't being mean. Mai was speaking the truth as she observed it. Many years later, after Mai had been exposed to Western television and values, she told me I was pretty. White wavy hair was now described as fashionable curly blond, and my faded eyes were a desired shade of blue.

Recently, while reminiscing, Mai pulled out a picture of David and me as we left Quảng Ngãi, standing at the top of mobile boarding stairs that had been wheeled up to the small plane on the tarmac. Mai didn't have a camera, so she must have asked someone at the Rehab

---

[35] In 2020 I bought a house with a back garden and terrace. Tiny blue blossoms appeared in the borders and around a tree. I thought about pulling them as weeds, but they were such a sweet looking plant, and I asked my garden expert sister-in-law what they were. She said they were an old-fashioned flower, forget-me-not. It had taken all those years to see forget-me-nots for the first time, long after Mai had introduced me to them.

Center for a copy. David had long sideburns, typical of the sixties, and I was wearing a blue "hippie" Indian shirt with embroidery on the front. Mai found the embroidery crude, certainly true when compared to the exquisitely fine technique of the Vietnamese and Mai's gifted pillow cover.

There we were, ready to board, an American couple leaving the most intense experience of our lives. I waved before ducking into the doorway. The plane flew over the rice fields and coastline. I had my final look at the landscape scarred by bomb craters. I was leaving behind my closest friend, my confidant, my sister. I didn't know if I would ever be in touch with her again.

Saigon and Letters and Poems

I'd always disliked Saigon, but it was a necessary stop to brief two new AFSC Saigon staff and connect to a flight out of Vietnam. Some enjoyed Saigon, particularly prior to 1974, with its wide, tree-lined streets and big city bustle. My visits seemed to coincide with the hottest days of the year when the humidity was most oppressive. Saigon was full of city-types living off the Americans. It was never a war zone. Journalists commuted to the war by hitching on American military vehicles and were back in town in time for cocktail hour at the Hotel Caravelle.

Like the house in Quảng Ngãi, the AFSC Saigon house was simple. It was situated in a modest neighborhood. The living room was plain, and we usually slept on a thin bamboo mat on the tiled floor, especially when it was hot; there was no air-conditioning. The living room connected to an open kitchen, where a cook made meals over a brazier. Walls and a tin roof separated the immaculate kitchen from the neighbors, but no one could prevent rats from coming in at night. I had slept here once before—during the "trip around the world" with the North and PRG delegation—and was bitten on the back by a rat. This was not a place to relax, have privacy, or be alone with my thoughts.

I had lost weight, and I asked a seamstress in Saigon to make a few clothes for the trip back to the States. There were no ready-made clothes in stores. We Western women with AFSC wore the same outfits as our female Vietnamese colleagues: simple black pants with elastic waistbands, topped by a collarless blouse, held together with snaps, not buttons. The use of snaps was a puzzle to me. With their exacting embroidery skills, Vietnamese women could easily create evenly spaced stitching around a buttonhole, and buttons held clothes more securely.

Vietnamese blouses bring back a searing image—one of my PTSD flashbacks—of the iconic Haeberle photograph from the My Lai massacre, the "Black Blouse Girl." A US soldier had ripped open the young woman's blouse as he was starting to rape her, yelling, "VC, boom, boom" (a slang expression for prostitute). In Haeberle's photo,[36] the woman on the right is cradling a child on her hip, her hand cupped on his bottom to hold him securely. She is looking down at her left hand, which is trying to do the impossible—close a snap on her blouse with just one hand.

In the foreground of the same photograph, an older woman attempts to shield those behind her. Moments earlier, she had been biting, kicking, and scratching the soldiers who attacked the black blouse woman. When Haeberle took the photograph, he interrupted the soldiers, who backed off, leaving the women to think they had been saved. But as Haeberle walked away, he heard multiple shots from M-60s. The women and children were murdered.

Writing this, I shiver. I can easily slide into the photograph and feel the terror and frustration of the young woman trying to align two parts of a snap to make it close. There is nothing I can do to save her. She isn't looking at the gun that would kill her and her baby. How could I erase her image from my mind as I leave Vietnam, returning to my country of buttons and zippers?

---

36   Ronald Haeberle was a US Army photographer who captured the horrific images of the murdered Vietnamese civilians on March 16, 1968, which were published in *Life* magazine and newspapers. Haeberle destroyed two photographs of easily identifiable US soldiers in the act of killing Vietnamese; only photographs of the Vietnamese victims were published.

Photo taken by Ronald Haeberle of woman in black blouse struggling to close snaps on her blouse. Moments later she is killed by U.S. soldier as part of the My Lai massacre

When the new clothes arrived, I put them in my leather bag. David and I had twin bags, one a slightly lighter brown than the other. They were soft imitation leather, and each had a shoulder strap. I was leaving Vietnam, bound for the US, with my only piece of luggage. As I was packing, I noticed a flap I hadn't seen before. It could be unsnapped to collapse the bag and create a secret compartment. I checked to see if David's bag had the same flap—yes—and there, I discovered folded letters written in Vietnamese on delicate, onionskin paper.

I speak Vietnamese but never learned to read or write it. Because the former director in Vietnam left as soon as David and I arrived, we didn't have the luxury of a two-month language and cultural training program, which other AFSC staff received. Vietnamese is a seven-tone language: one word can have seven different meanings depending on the speaker's tone. Without language classes, I learned to speak as a child would—mimicking and repeating phrases. By learning on the street, so to speak, I picked up the accent of the local, coastal people of Quảng Ngãi Province. Sometimes people joked that I spoke as if I had saltwater in my mouth. Imagine a Caucasian woman speaking in the distinct regional twang! I read the newspaper aloud to myself, pronouncing each word according to the diacritical symbol over it. By hearing the words, I understood them.

The only way I could decipher the letters pulled from David's suitcase was to read them aloud. As my mind flashed back to Kiem and David in the bomb shelter, I wondered if they were love letters. *Is he working for the CIA? Why is he hiding these secret letters?* The room started to close around me. I had to get out of the house to read them. I wanted to escape the heat, pain, and banging in my head.

I thought about taking AFSC's copy of a Vietnamese-English dictionary, but it was five inches thick, too bulky for my backpack. Besides, it could be missed. I made excuses and left.

My goal was to find a place to read in private. Saigon had many more coffee shops than Quảng Ngãi, but I didn't know which might be safe. In general, it was our policy to stay away from cafés or restaurants where government officials might gather to socialize or spend money. In Quảng Ngãi, explosives were detonated several times at such venues. Once, a movie theater opened and immediately closed after a homemade bomb blew up, injuring fifty-seven people and killing four. The movie was a government documentary, and the average person couldn't afford a ticket. Those privileged enough to attend became targets of anti-government forces.

It was too hot to walk far, but I found a café, shaded by a tree, and ordered coffee, a drink I could linger over. There is a ritual to make Vietnamese coffee. A *phin*, a metal device holding ground coffee, is balanced on the rim of a cup, and hot water, poured over the grounds, creates an aromatic brew, drop by drop. Finally, sweet evaporated milk is added. I tried to steady my hands. They were sweaty, and I didn't want to smear the writing.

It only took one letter to understand they were all from Kiem, full of flowery phrases and professions of love. One was a poem about lovers separated by land but united by the moon in the sky. I could taste bile in my mouth. I was overwhelmed. I walked back to the AFSC house and put the letters in the hidden compartment of my suitcase, hoping David wouldn't notice, until I could find more time to read.

Even though it was still morning, I hoped I might sleep. My skin stuck to the sheets. The electricity, which could have operated a small fan, was on the blink. I tried to imagine snow and recall happy years when I skied in the White Mountains or Vermont. Though these pleasant images didn't cool me, they brought some mental relief. But nothing made the pain go away.

The next day, when I checked David's bag, the letters were gone. The following day, we went to the Saigon airport and boarded a plane to Malaysia. I was leaving a place and people I had come to love, despite war. But the relationship I had with my husband was in jeopardy. David and I had started anew in Vietnam—but once again, we lost each other.

CHAPTER 10

Return to US and Antiwar Work

I had booked an itinerary for what was supposed to be a wonderful adventure home. Some AFSC team members returned to the United States via Bhutan and Nepal, but I wanted a more southern route to Sri Lanka and Africa. David had traveled as part of a youth delegation and a Peace Corps trainer in several West African countries, and he was curious to visit East Africa, an academic interest during graduate school. I hoped to see a childhood Quaker friend and his family in Kenya. We'd be traveling for two months.

We went to a remote oceanside beach in Malaysia with a few simple cottages. The sandy beach was narrow, with coconut trees reaching close to the water.

David and I barely conversed. We didn't talk about his affair with Kiem. We didn't speak about Vietnam or all we had left behind. After a few days of sun and swimming, we sought intimacy. Though I was angry, I also felt alone, stripped of my work and friends. I wanted the comfort that comes from sex. I had always been attracted to David physically, but now I was repelled. Not only had he been romantically—and maybe sexually—involved with Mai's best friend, he was unable to have sex with me. He must have felt guilt, some form of grief. At the same time, I was numb from his betrayal and disoriented from abruptly leaving a war zone. I didn't try to explore my feelings. I was still sick and mentally weak.

Despite our estrangement, we followed our itinerary like zombies:

the Seychelles, Sri Lanka, Kenya, Tanzania, Egypt. We observed extraordinary tropical fish while scuba diving in the Indian Ocean around the Seychelles. In Sri Lanka we watched students rehearse at a traditional dance school. In Egypt I pictured my father visiting archeological digs on his Indian Chief motorcycle when he was my age. Africa was so big, with its enormous sky and open spaces. I could stretch my arms wide and not touch anyone or anything—vastly different from the condensed style of Vietnamese tropical living. And the whole time, I was holding my breath.

Returning to the USA

We ended our travels in Spain, where we met my parents. They had booked rooms in elegant paradors, former castles converted to hotels. The highlight was Granada, with its Moorish influence, which fascinated my father because of the time he had spent in Middle Eastern countries and his fondness for Arab culture. And my mother always threw herself wholeheartedly into new adventures.

My parents continued to travel, and David and I flew back to the US. After landing at JFK airport, his brother, Peter, took us sightseeing, including a ride on the Staten Island Ferry. Who were these odd-looking people? After being in a country of homogeneous people, dark-haired and petite, I was stunned at the sights around me. I'm sure many Vietnam veterans suffer the same coming-home shock. I recall a man in patent-leather heels and a red velvet coat. Was it his height? His enormous girth? There were no fat Vietnamese during the war. Velvet in the summer? His feminine shoes? American popular culture had shifted in ways that surprised me.

Like other AFSC team members, I had worn Ho Chi Minh sandals, with crude soles made from a section of a tire. The rubber was thick and the edges rough. Now the people moving around me wore shoes in a myriad of materials, from leather to canvas. It was confusing.

Ho Chi Minh sandals made from rubber tire

Drugstores were overwhelming. Stuffed animals, flashlights, nail polish—and choices for cold relief stretched half an aisle. I couldn't bear going into these stores for months.

We were in New York City with skyscrapers and thousands of people of every description. My worst meltdown occurred when I attended a ballet at Lincoln Center. David's mother, a trained ballet dancer, was born in St. Petersburg, Russia, and Peter suggested we secure tickets to a performance of a Russian ballet troupe. When I was a child, my father took me—just me—to a ballet performance while my mother and brother were away, and the joy of discovering dancers who walked on their toes is one of my first memories.

At first, it was wonderful to be in Lincoln Center. No bombs—just a familiar, peaceful murmuring of the audience finding their seats and the orchestra tuning. But as the ballet dancers leaped and flew through the air, I started to sob. I was thinking of Kiem, her stories of dancing in a cultural troupe, unfettered and happy, but now trapped in a steel brace. Fierce, mixed emotions. I also hated her and my husband for betraying me. And then my mind went to the tortured prisoners chained to beds in the prison ward at Quảng Ngãi Hospital. They weren't flying free. These thoughts almost made me black out.

I was sitting in Lincoln Center while they suffered. How could I have left them behind? I stood up and bumped, ducked, and shuffled to escape the hall.

Survivor's Guilt

My reserved, New England parents discouraged "scenes." When I attended Friends Meetings for Worship, we sat in silence. There wasn't even music. Yet this particular evening, those rules of behavior dissolved. I sobbed and sobbed.

David and Peter were solicitous, but I couldn't explain my feelings. Later, I became aware of "survivor's guilt." Many American veterans were never normal again. Guilt and suffering drove some to commit suicide or become homeless. I was a survivor, but my friends were back in Vietnam, many without limbs, and innocent people were locked in the interrogation compound or hospital.

The day after the ballet, David and I went to the ABC studios of *Good Morning America* to be interviewed about the torture of political prisoners I had documented in Vietnam. ABC had enlarged my photographs. To my shock, the interviewer only wanted quick soundbites. I hadn't prepared a statement, and the television anchors led me down rabbit holes that weren't on point. Speed, that was what the US was about. No nuance or history. Just a few words. Nothing more. I was shaken but determined to be ready next time.

I also had an epiphany. My eyewitness accounts and photographs of prisoners were "hot" news. I was familiar enough with journalism and media to know I had to move quickly when there was interest. For months, AFSC staffers Diane and Michael Jones had documented the role of mercenary South Korean soldiers, on the US payroll, who committed forty-five separate incidents of civilian massacres—thirteen involving the killing of over a hundred women, children, and old men in the Quảng Ngãi area. The death toll vastly outnumbered that of My Lai, yet Diane and Michael generated little media attention. I was not going to let this opportunity to advocate for Mai and the prisoners slip by. I prepared answers for interviews going forward.

AFSC and Amnesty International suggested a cross-country speaking tour across the United States for David and me. Though our relationship was strained, we remained bonded through our mutual commitment. The opportunity to talk about my experiences and be heard by receptive audiences was healing. I avoided a repeat of the emotional trauma experienced at Lincoln Center because I was taking an active role in freeing those prisoners, helping to end the war that had injured my Vietnamese friends. I was their voice. Many Vietnam veterans returning to the US experienced a void, nothing to connect them to their prior horrific experiences. Talking about mine was therapeutic.

Mai told a story that illustrates the untenable position of American soldiers and the subtle, nonviolent form of power that was typically Vietnamese.

> The US soldiers sometimes thought the little "urchins" hanging around the military bases were cute, naïve waifs. The soldiers might give them candy or small change. But, these children, though they had no power over the soldiers, were not passive. They would pretend to teach American soldiers how to count in Vietnamese by pointing to each of the five fingers on one hand and chanting one syllable words: đả đảo đế quốc Mỹ. The words were short and sounded as if they could be numbers, but if pronounced with the correct tones, the children were teaching the soldiers to say, "Overthrow the American imperialists."

Life in Vietnam could be confusing.

For many of us who saw the war up close, memories can remain bottled up until they explode or wither away. I was fortunate to be able to share what I had witnessed and suffered. AFSC director Lou Kubica, whose position I inherited, became a Buddhist priest. Some team members reentered society; others retreated to farms. Two AFSC doctors retired early to live off the grid—one in Vermont and one in Nebraska. A former head of the physical therapy program, who had become quite deaf, lives alone, without phone or email. If you want to contact her, you have to write a letter.

The Question of Torture

David and I spent the next year sharing our experiences with the American public. The US government was still creating a media frenzy over the return of American POWS, and it was a timely opportunity to remind Americans about Vietnamese political prisoners. We spoke to peace groups, churches, newspaper editorial boards, journalists, college radio DJs, in-home gatherings, and packed auditoriums. We showed clips from *A Question of Torture*. The film crew interviewed and photographed prisoners in Vietnam, including two paralyzed POWs rehabilitated at the AFSC Center.

I advocated for the release of all prisoners in Vietnam, not just the two in the film. It was my wish that these men could go home to their prior life. Ironically, one of them later stepped on a mine on the path to his house and was killed; the other reconciled with his brothers who were both in the South Vietnamese army. Every time I gave a talk, I thought of Mai and hoped she was safe. Did she know I was speaking for her and the others I had left behind?

David and I brought new information to the American public. It had not occurred to many that Vietnamese men and women were also held as POWS, not to mention thousands unjustly imprisoned for their beliefs.

Only twice during the war years were Americans exposed to images of Vietnamese prisoners in "tiger cages." The first appeared in the July 7, 1970, issue of *Life*. One photograph documented a Buddhist monk looking through the bars of a cage on Con Son Island. The photos were taken by future US Senator Tom Harkin, who uncovered the secret of the cages with Don Luce, an employee of the World Council of Churches. My photograph of two prisoners, released from the cages in 1973, documented that this inhumane practice had continued, even after the exposure by *Life* and a congressional investigation. What did it take to make Americans confront this issue? I had photos and documentation for the prisoners held in Quảng Ngãi. I was a firsthand observer, a woman who spoke Vietnamese and lived in Vietnam longer than most American soldiers.

The next phase of the tour was in France, the Netherlands, and Germany. In Paris, Father Thi organized a large gathering of expatriate Vietnamese. They were amused to hear us speaking Vietnamese with our country accents. A murmur went through the crowd when they saw nostalgic pictures of rice paddies or crabs *ut muoi* (with cracked salt and pepper). We spoke French with the media and presented to audiences around Paris.

My favorite part was going to the Netherlands. A young Dutch couple who was active in the antiwar movement hosted us in Amsterdam. The maternal side of my family is Dutch, and I feel an affinity to them. The Dutch spend their lives pushing back the sea, nearly a third of the land. When I was eight years old and my Dutch-born grandmother was living with us, she kept us abreast of the 1953 breach of dikes in Holland and the destruction of land and people. The Dutch understood the generations required to create dikes. Killing the people was bad enough, but why did they have to ruin the land for future generations by destroying the thousand-year-old dikes in Vietnam?

Our last lap was in Germany. The atmosphere was different. We spoke on the stage at Berlin's Free University with representatives of antiwar groups. Among the speakers were members of the Red Army Faction, a far-left group that would become violent and responsible for dozens of assassinations and bombings. There were thousands in the outdoor park where we made our presentation. Young people hosted us for a couple nights. I liked seeing how Germans my age lived—their furniture, interior colors, coffee makers.

David and I were also key witnesses at a German trial. Our testimony was sought by an antiwar group to justify a large demonstration calling for the release of Vietnamese political prisoners. A policeman had been injured by a protester on trial for the assault. Our role wasn't to address the action of the police or protestor but to give evidence supporting the justification for the demonstration—Vietnamese political prisoners were being tortured. The trial was at a large castle outside Berlin, an obstacle for public observers who wished to attend. There were five judges, per the German judicial system, no jury, and a courtroom filled with spectators, mostly protesters who had attended the demonstration.

At one point, someone stood up and shouted antiwar slogans. Police with high, black leather boots and hats with visors rushed into the room with batons and German shepherds. The room was cleared, except for us and the judges. We sat, a bit unnerved, waiting. The trial never resumed. We left the castle and flew back to the US.

We received the tragic news that our teammate Rick and the wife of social worker Trung had died in a civilian airplane crash during a terrible storm. It was hard not to be in Vietnam to comfort Trung and prepare for Rick's burial.

Father and Mother

I discovered things my parents had held back while I was in Vietnam. My mother had been diagnosed with cancer. And my intelligent, handsome father had been treated for depression and alcoholism. During the next year, my mother declined while my father drank. I flew to Boston to see them as often as possible. When I learned my mother was terminal, the director of the AFSC office rejected my request for two weeks off, instead giving me a directive for a more generous leave. At the ancient age of fifty, he was older and wiser than me. He exclaimed, "Jane, go home for as long as you need. You will never see your mother again."

We couldn't depend on my father to help. He had found a way to access medications, combining drugs with alcohol. His behavior became erratic. One day I found him unconscious on the garage floor in his silk, paisley bathrobe, lying on oil stains, genitals exposed. My brother and I thought it was best to commit him to a psychiatric institution, Harvard University's McLean Hospital, where he had been hospitalized while I was in Vietnam. He managed to contact his attorney, and the four of us traveled to McLean in the same car. Once there, he and his attorney claimed he wasn't a danger to himself, and McLean refused to admit him.

But the intervention seemed to take my father back from the brink. He got sober. He read poetry to my mother as her health continued its downward spiral. An hour before she died, she wanted to get out of bed, but my father told her gently that it would be dangerous. Her last words were "Well, can't I just dangle my feet?"

My father would use drugs and alcohol to kill himself five months later.

Indochina Peace Campaign: Jane Fonda

When we returned to the US, David and I went to visit his parents in Laguna Beach, California. The phone rang, and it was Jane Fonda asking to speak to me. Jane and her husband, Tom Hayden, were living in Santa Monica, about an hour away. She said they had read some of my Vietnam reports in the *Los Angeles Times* and *New York Times* and wanted to meet me.

Because I had grown up without a television, with parents who were academics and not interested in popular culture, I wasn't sure who Jane Fonda was. I had never seen her movies. Plus, I was in Vietnam when Jane was politically active, so I was unaware of her antiwar activities. I had heard of her father, Henry Fonda, though, and decided it would be interesting to visit her. David and I drove to Santa Monica in his parents' giant 1970 Buick on multilaned freeways. What a contrast to travel in Quảng Ngãi.

Jane and Tom shared a modest house with another couple, Carol Kurtz and Jack Nichols, near the beach. From our first visit, we engaged in lively discussion about the war, and I returned several times to show Jane my photographs of Vietnamese women who had been tortured. She asked if I would let Indochina Peace Campaign (IPC), the organization she and Tom founded, publish some in its magazine.[37]

David and I became involved in the next phase of IPC's effort, *Stop Funding the War*, a strategy developed by Tom. Under the brilliant planning of IPC organizer Larry Levin and soft-spoken but determined Ed Snyder, executive director of Friends National Committee on Legislation (FCNL), David and I visited the most critical congressional members whose votes were needed to halt the $474 million appropriations for South Vietnam's Thieu government. We spent several months in Washington, DC, at IPC offices in the National Council of Churches building, across from the Supreme Court. David and I were lodged at the William Penn House (currently Friends Place) on Capitol Hill. I thought I'd escaped the heat of Vietnam, but without air-conditioning or fans, the house was hot on those summer evenings when we gathered with other guests and staff to watch the Watergate hearings on a black-and-white television set.

AFSC offered me a position on the Peace Team in San Francisco, and David accepted a position with the Indochina Resource Center in Berkley. It was my first trip by land across the country. I was impressed by its geographic wonders and vast spaces. I wondered, if Mai had seen for herself the size and power of the US, would she have been intimidated? I don't think so.

David and I lived in the maid's quarters of the AFSC offices, in a former grand Victorian house, until we settled into a second-floor apartment. Within a few months, I went on speaking trips with Jane Fonda and singer-activist Holly Near. I used to say, "Jane was the

---

37   Earlier that year, Jane and Tom had organized a multicity tour to educate Americans about the 200,000 political prisoners being held in South Vietnam. In addition to Jane and Tom, two of their friends were also speakers: Bob Chenoweth, an American POW, and John-Pierre Dubris, an elementary school teacher from France who was imprisoned for two years in Saigon. The tour culminated with events in the US, and other parts of the world, during International Days of Concern with Saigon's political prisoners, September 16–23, 1973.

draw, I was the information, and Holly was the emotion." Jane enjoyed calling my office switchboard, saying, "This is Jane calling for Jane."

Sometimes Jane stayed at our apartment if the three of us were scheduled for an event in San Francisco. She slept in the study on a blow-up mattress. Often, we would go out to a café where Jane ordered "real French coffee." I never envied her celebrity. There were several occasions when people would rudely—and sometimes crudely—speak to her. As our friendship developed, I was startled to observe Jane's insecurities. She had a deep sense of injustice but looked to Tom for direction. Sometimes she even asked me what I thought she should say at a forthcoming speaking engagement. Over time, Jane gained her own sense of self-worth.[38]

Jane Fonda and the Indochina Peace Campaign (IPC)

---

38   When I last saw Jane at Tom Hayden's memorial service in 2017, she told me she was devoting herself full-time to activism and giving up men. She has found her confidence, and I admire the environmental work she is doing.

CHAPTER 11

End of the War

Letters

Between 1973 and 1975, Mai and I corresponded frequently, and I saved her letters in a three-ring binder. I occasionally needed help translating them and had sections, or whole letters, translated mainly by Vietnamese employees at a local nail salon. I was sensitive to their political persuasion and which parts I asked them to translate. Some were virulent anti-Communists, and reading the words of a guerrilla fighter might offend them.

Collage of envelopes from letters sent by Mai to Jane

Mai, like many Vietnamese, has an inextricable bond to poetry, which is evident in her letters. Thousands of years of war kept the Vietnamese culture focused on easily portable arts such as music and poetry. Folk and classical poetry exist side by side. Almost every schoolchild knows the epic narrative poem *The Tale of Kieu*, adventures of a beautiful woman who sacrifices herself for her family. That a book-length poem is a cultural icon underscores the value of poetry in Vietnamese culture. Mai may have only had an eighth-grade education, but she expresses herself in lyrical, moving words.

Liberation in Quảng Ngãi

In 1974 the war was ending, and I thought I might meet Mai again. ABC television approached AFSC to ask if David and I would join a crew headed to Vietnam to film the tense situation as the North Vietnamese Army and PRG gained territory and strength in South Vietnam.

First, I spoke at a conference in the Netherlands about foreign adoption. It was controversial. I questioned the selling of babies of color to mainly childless White couples, framing it as an imperialist initiative to remove children from countries that couldn't protect or provide for them. David arrived on the last day of the conference, and we were watching television with Dutch friends when the liberation of Saigon was announced. We rejoiced in the news and were stunned the North Vietnamese and PRG had won so quickly. Where was Mai and the AFSC team? Would ABC's plan change regarding the television crew?

I was glad to have David in my life at that moment. He was my link to Vietnam, and I was proud of our working partnership there and on the grueling speaking tours. I was sharing this happiness with someone who understood and admired the struggle of the Vietnamese people. There were few civilians like us.

The next day, on our way to Paris, the AFSC international division director told us the trip with ABC was canceled. It was impossible for civilian planes to land in Vietnam. He also reported the Quaker Service team was safe. They had flown to Saigon and were staying in the AFSC house there. What he didn't mention was that Quảng Ngãi had been liberated almost two weeks earlier. While we were celebrating Saigon's liberation, Mai had already experienced hers. When the AFSC team left, they put Mai in charge of the house in Quảng Ngãi.

The liberation of Quảng Ngãi had not caused a single casualty, but fleeing ARVN troops created chaos and fighting outside the city, resulting in hundreds of deaths. Earl Martin, a Mennonite volunteer staying with Mai at the AFSC house, wrote:[39]

> Monday, March 24, 1975, Daytime
> *There was no fighting near Quảng Ngãi. Yet suddenly the ARVN military troops began to confiscate military trucks and jeeps and went barreling down the street. It set off a major panic. People tried to jump onto these vehicles or hang on to the sides of the trucks. Police were fleeing in any possible vehicle. The fear of the unknown and what would happen to those who had supported the US and South Vietnamese government created a stampede. Even the guards at the interrogation compound panicked and set fires in the center of the building to burn documents. No longer locked behind sets of gates, prisoners fled the interrogation compound. Meanwhile, civilians sensed the uncertain atmosphere, and many of them joined the exodus. It became a crazy evacuation. People weren't thinking; they were just fleeing. The trucks were jammed and layered with people.*

I later had an opportunity to ask Quy, who had directed the prosthetic work at the AFSC Rehab Center, why he fled. He said he wasn't afraid of the revolution, but "I was afraid of subjecting my family to being injured during a battle to take over the city. Ironically,

---

39 Earl Martin, *Reaching the Other Side*, Crown Publisher, NY, 1978, p. 89. Description of panic of people leaving the city.

that battle never took place, and we risked our lives trying to flee." In 2000, his wife, Phong, told me a story that nearly matches Earl's:[40]

> The truck beds were so full that babies were crushed to death. It was like they were animals in a stampede. Just rushing madly in the night. When we got to Chu Lai, people fought madly to get onto one of the ships. . . . Old people and children got trampled in the water. Someone threw a rope down from the deck to the shore. A mother with three children tried to climb up the rope, but she dropped one of her children, who fell into the water. . . . There was nothing she could do. A lot of soldiers pushed their way onto the ship. . . . Other soldiers who couldn't get aboard threw grenades to wipe out a layer of people so they could climb to the top. Then they tossed the dead bodies into the water. . . . By the end, the last people trying to escape didn't have to wade through water. They just walked over a ramp of bodies. It was so terrible. I didn't even try to get on the ship. We spent the night huddled in the rice paddies. Soldiers had stripped off their uniforms and were begging for civilian clothing. Then at dawn the bo doi [NLF cadre] came out announcing that all of Quảng Ngãi Province was liberated and there would be no reprisals.

Mai told me the night of liberation was quiet. She'd been left in charge of the AFSC house, with the Vietnamese staff that lived there, plus Earl Martin, who asked if he could stay at the house because it had a stronger bunker. Earl and his family had lived in Vietnam for several years, working with refugees and later managing a mine-clearing operation. He recorded a detailed chronology of events at the AFSC house:[41]

---

40 Ibid, pp. 124–125. Phuong's description of people fleeing on a US ship.
41 Ibid, p. 94. Earl observing Mai's pleasure at the liberation of the city.

About 2 a.m., I was awakened to the voices of three bo doi who had come into the city and were standing just outside the Quaker house. They were saying, "Hello, friends. You need to run no more. Peace has come to Quảng Ngãi. Just stay calmly where you are. Tomorrow more bo doi will bring tanks into town to guarantee your security."

I rushed to wake everyone up. Mai was already strapping on her legs. Mai asked me, her voice snapping with excitement, "Did they see you?"

I went into the street and talked with the NLF cadre and the neighbors who were chatting excitedly.

"Impressive, weren't they? So peaceful it all was. No fighting. No shelling. No bombing. They just walked right into town."

Watching the drama unfold, back at the gate of the house facing the street, Mai was beaming with pride. She exuded the quiet ecstasy of a drama director who has just witnessed her actors perform a stunning coup de theater. Mai commented to me, "Nice-looking fellows, weren't they?"

Mai told me how her comrades arrived in town.

It was a crazy time for me. Comrades from my years with the NLF arrived in Quảng Ngãi. They asked people on the street for someone named Thuy. They didn't know that I had taken the alias "Mai." It took a while to sort out the confusion, but soon I was hugging and laughing with a couple of old friends. Some of the cadre had never met me, but they had been part of a communications network with me.

Earl described dinner that night.

I had met a young man named Trong two days before, and he also arrived at the house to join the crowd. Trong and I were sitting at a big table, sharing dinner, and at one point he asked me, "When am I going to meet this Thuy we've all been hearing so much about?"

I responded, "Well, we could possibly arrange to have you meet her one of these days. In fact, Trong, Thuy, or Mai, as we call her, is sitting across the table from you."

Trong raised his eyebrows and smiled at Mai. He turned to Mai and asked, "What do you think of the way we liberated Quảng Ngãi? Pretty clever, wouldn't you say?"

"Clever?" Mai's eyes danced at the opportunity to fence with a comrade. "Doesn't look to me like you did very much. You just said, 'Boo,' and the ARVN tucked tail and fled."

After a bit more give and take, Mai continued her teasing.

"What I can't figure out is why you all were so poorly prepared. When I was still in the hills, I remember how we prepared for the Tet Offensive. Flags, lots of flags, propaganda leaflets, announcement bills, the works."

Trong responded, "That's because when we took the first step, the enemy got very frightened and withdrew. That was only last week. After that, it all went so fast. The morale of the ARVN just collapsed. Events went faster than we anticipated. We had to run to keep up!" [42]

May 1975: Celebrating in Paris

During this tumultuous time in Vietnam, David and I went from Amsterdam to Paris with antiwar Dutch friends to share a French meal and toast the peace. We met with friends in the French chapter of the Union of Vietnamese, a nonprofit organization for Vietnamese living outside Vietnam. They insisted we come to a large victory

---

42   Ibid, pp. 110-111. Description of conversation between Mai and newly arrived cadre Anh Trong.

celebration. There were at least 5,000 Vietnamese at the Théâtre des Champs-Elysées. The gathering opened with five minutes of silence for those who died in Vietnam. Tears of sadness and joy ran down our cheeks. We listened to liberation songs and speeches and watched dance performances. The highlight was a victory speech by a representative of the conservative Vietnamese Catholic missionary community in France. The entire political and economic spectrum of Vietnamese in France was represented, from women who came to France as servants of French Army officers to wealthy Vietnamese women in sequined velvet *áo dàis* and men in suits or the traditional tunic dress. It was a remarkable step toward a unified community in a spirit of peace and reconciliation.

What a wonderful and confusing time. The PRG embassy was dissolving. Communications between the former and new officials were being sorted out. David and I wished to assure the PRG that AFSC was prepared to continue to fund the Rehab Center in Quảng Ngãi. Representatives of the PRG, including Ambassador Dinh Ba Thi, stated they were anxious to cooperate with us "as twins." A formal proposal approved by AFSC was presented to the PRG delegation with enthusiastic response. Also, David and I wished to secure permission to travel to Vietnam to film and document the real situation, to rebut the warnings by some media sources that there would be a bloodbath. AFSC wanted to pursue an educational opportunity to create understanding and goodwill. Although everyone was keen to continue AFSC involvement in Vietnam, there were many logistical obstacles and different perspectives among the Vietnamese. The Vietnamese officials assured us that they hoped AFSC could continue to be of help, but now that Vietnam was an independent country and there was peace, it was also time for them to direct their own affairs. There was a lot of back-and-forth between David and me in Paris and AFSC Philadelphia headquarters. We waited patiently for answers. After a few weeks, we decided to return to the US, and hopefully decisions would reach us there.

Summer 1975: Quảng Ngãi

Back in Quảng Ngãi, Mai was given a role on the NLF Board of Inquiry.

> My job was to interview ARVN soldiers, police, and other officials who had supported the South Vietnamese government. If I felt these individuals could come to accept and work with the new government, I released them. If I believed they were incorrigible, I sent them for classes and education. Each day someone would come on a motorbike to take me to the building where the interviews took place. I didn't know if people got too busy to transport me, but soon the driver started to come infrequently. Gradually, the driver no longer appeared. I assumed I had been replaced on the Inquiry Board, though no one ever communicated about my status.
>
> I was mesmerized by all that was happening in my country. I listened to the radio and read news reports about the exciting changes, especially in Saigon. It was a monumental moment in Vietnam's long history of its struggle for independence. Generations of my family had sacrificed for this moment. I decided to take a bus to Saigon, knowing I could meet my AFSC colleagues there and stay at the house. I wanted to see the situation for myself. Saigon is where the action was happening, and there would never be a time like this.
>
> I didn't drink for two days because I wasn't sure how easily I could find an accessible bathroom on the long trip from Quảng Ngãi to Saigon. Saigon was such a huge place. The roads were packed, yet everyone seemed calm. The AFSC team was excited to see me, and I took turns riding on the back of one of their bicycles, observing changes. Many students had been recruited to collect ARVN weapons, and the schoolyards were piled high with discarded weapons. By now, the initial panic had diminished, and it was remarkable to watch the young

people raised under the South Vietnamese government's regime meeting NLF or North Vietnamese soldiers their own age. The locals and soldiers chatted in a friendly manner. Each had many questions for the other. Some of the young NLF or North Vietnamese soldiers who had spent months or years in the jungle were, like me, wide-eyed at the biggest and busiest city they had ever seen—if they had even been in a city.

Paul Quinn-Judge, a Brit on the AFSC staff, told me an amusing story about a trip to the main Saigon post office, where he had intended to send a cable to Philadelphia headquarters. Outside, a young *bo doi* was looking helpless. He couldn't find the bicycle he had left against the wall. A betel nut vendor squatting nearby scolded him: "You aren't in the mountains anymore, kiddo. You should know better. In Saigon you could even have your bike stolen while you are riding it. Never leave it unattended, country boy!"

1975 Fall: Quảng Ngãi

After Mai returned to Quảng Ngãi, she went back to her job at the AFSC Rehabilitation Center. The new government assigned a North Vietnamese doctor as director. Mai and the former AFSC Vietnamese staff were impressed by the government's action.

> Doctors were scarce, and to immediately have a fully trained Vietnamese doctor on staff boosted our morale. During the war, no Vietnamese doctor ever set foot inside the Rehab Center.

The war's end also meant Mai could begin to track down her family and guerrilla friends. How she found her husband, Ly, is a remarkable story.

I still hadn't heard from my husband. It had been nearly ten years. This wasn't uncommon during the war, especially if families were separated. Yet now that the war was over, I still held out hope that he would make his way home. I couldn't help but wonder if he had been killed or was perhaps recuperating in a hospital in the north.

Seven months after liberation, I was reading the newspaper when I ran across something unusual. A person with the same name, Ly, as my husband and the same engineering profession was preparing to run for the National Assembly. My head swirled, and I almost lost my breath with the joy of knowing he might be alive. But then I said to myself, "How could this be? Could my husband have returned from the North and not contacted me? How could he be so well established in just a few months that he is now well enough to run for national office? No, no, it couldn't be—just a highly unusual coincidence."

Still, I thought, since the name of the company that employed Mr. Ly was mentioned in the article, I would send a letter to this workplace. After many years of sorrow, I felt hope and excitement. I wasn't prepared for the hurt that followed. Just a week later, a woman came to my reception desk at the Rehabilitation Center and introduced herself as Ly's sister. I had met her once before, but she looked different now—much older.

I asked her, "Where is Ly? Surely you didn't come alone, did you?"

"No," she told me, "Ly is waiting outside. I am bringing a request from him."

I was elated and puzzled. I didn't have any idea what was going on, but I asked my supervisor if I could take the rest of the afternoon off. I asked Ly and his sister to follow me as I rode on the back of a hired motorcycle. When we got to the house, I slid off the cycle as gracefully as possible and invited them into the little house that the government had recently issued to me as a war victim. I was moved to see my husband, but he remained impassive.

Once we were in the house, he didn't even wait until I served the traditional tea before presenting me with a divorce agreement. Ly said, "I want you to sign this because you can't have any children."

Maybe he said more words than that, but those words were all I remembered. I was outraged. My sentiment toward him turned to anger. I demanded, "And how do you know I can't have children? What proof do you have? You are horribly cruel. You're rejecting me because I have lost my legs, not because I can't have children. This is not the revolution's philosophy. We all sacrificed together. You have lost touch with the women who were left behind during the war. I might not be physically stronger than before my accident, but I am mentally more able than before. There is joy in regaining one's life with artificial limbs. I am not handicapped, and I can have a child. I am totally convinced!" Ly and his sister left abruptly, and I was still fuming.

It took Ly a while to regain his courage to visit me again. A few months later, he and his sister came to my house early one evening. I was still incensed and said to Ly, "If you had lost your legs, I would not desert you. In my work at the Rehab Center, I saw with my own eyes, many times disabled people can bear children. I still have my monthly menstrual cycles. There is no reason why I can't have a baby."

I used all the motivational techniques I had learned as a provincial propaganda officer. A torrent of words flowed out of my mouth, snot from my nose, and tears from my eyes. All those years of waiting and pent-up anger and frustration poured out. I waited. Ly didn't respond. In desperation, I pleaded, "Give me two months, and I can prove to you that I can have children like any other woman. I am your wife."

That snake didn't take up my challenge, and my only revenge, at that time, was that I did not give him the divorce he was seeking. But do you know, a year later, that man went ahead and married someone else? I learned that he was holding a fairly important political office in Danang. Maybe he was planning on climbing to a high position in the National Assembly, but he had committed bigamy, and I could bring him down from his ladder if I wanted.

Within a year, the new government moved the Rehabilitation Center. The new director felt patients could be better served in a more substantial structure built by Canadians in Qui Nhon, three hours away by car. Mai was ready.

We'd been well trained, believed our work was worthwhile, and wanted to keep our jobs, but most of us had lived our whole lives in or near Quảng Ngãi. It was a bit traumatic to move, but I looked forward to the future eagerly and embraced the change.

During the next few years, letters between Mai and me were returned as we had both changed residences. We lost complete touch.

CHAPTER 12

Losing Touch: Thirty-Five Years Without Contact

1980s

The years passed, and suddenly thirty-five years disappeared. Family life was absorbing. David and I remained together and had returned to our areas of academic training. Our daughter, Maria Mai, was born in the Year of the Tiger in San Francisco. My work continued at AFSC, while David worked for a think tank and publisher, Indochina Resource Center. We moved to Washington, DC, where David held a position with the House Foreign Affairs Committee. I finished a master's degree, was awarded a National Endowment for the Arts Fellowship in arts management, and published a book on a specialized type of Japanese resist-dyed textile, shibori.[43] In 1984, now with a second child, Nicholas, we lived in Stockholm, Sweden, for three years. I was employed at the Museum of Far Eastern Antiquities, and David was a fellow at the Stockholm International Peace Research Institute (SIPRI). I tried to notify Mai of my changes of address but never received any letters. Later, Mai told me she hadn't gotten any either.

During those years in Europe, we traveled as a family, especially in Italy and France, with summer weeks in Corsica and winter holidays skiing in Austria and Norway. When we came back to Washington, DC, David returned to work in Congress, and I became director of the Woodrow Wilson House Museum, a property of the National Trust

---

43   Barton, Jane with Yoshiko Wada and Mary Kellogg Rice, *Shibori: The Inventive Art of Japanese Shaped Resist Dyeing*, Tokyo, Kodansha, 2012.

for Historic Preservation. One hot late afternoon, I took the children swimming. While I watched them, I opened our mail. One letter was from a staffer for an important US senator. Her note informed me that she'd been having an affair with David.

Once again, my world turned upside down. David's other affairs had happened before we had children, but now that we had responsibility for two incredible human beings, I couldn't forgive him. I filed for divorce. The process dragged on.

Over the next year-and-a-half, I had multiple addresses. Mai and I wrote to each other without success. I have a copy of a letter Mai kept after it was returned to her stamped "Address: Not Known" on the outside of the envelope. She sent another to Connecticut, to "Plant Street" instead of "Plant Court." It never reached me. In Vietnam, streets are streets. I barely knew my own address during those painful years.

1990s

After returning from Sweden, I was chief curator and preservation officer of the US Treasury Building, a historic landmark next to the White House. Barbara Bush was the honorary chair of the Preservation Committee, and at a luncheon to launch the effort to raise private funds, President Bush and I addressed the fifty guests. I presented slides to this gathering of influential and high-net-worth individuals, explaining plans to restore the federal landmark to its original glory.

The job carried me into the world of Washington's elite. I interacted and met with Presidents Ronald Reagan, George H.W. Bush, and Bill Clinton. I socialized with senior government officials, in particular as a guest of Secretary of Treasury Nicholas Brady and his wife Katherine ("Kitty") at their house on the Eastern Shore and in their New York City apartment.

As I was meeting influential people as part of my job, I couldn't help but have high expectations for stimulating, brilliant conversations, but often my encounters were disappointing. President and Barbara Bush and the Bradys invited me to a private breakfast to thank me for the completion of several preservation projects. The four of them had previously visited Paul Mellon at his Kentucky farm, where another guest, Queen Elizabeth, boarded some of her horses. The women talked about the Queen's jewels, and President Bush told a story about his dog, Millie, throwing up in the White House hall. Then President Bush turned to me and said, "Of course, you heard about my memorable vomiting event in Japan, right? I always say, like father, like son." I didn't bother to point out that Millie was female.

During those years, I mused about the irony of my working for the same government, though with different leadership, that had waged the war on Vietnam. And where was Mai now? Were some of her family alive? Did she reunite with them? Did she find love?

As for me, I was adrift. My life had been dedicated, for most of my adult life, to Vietnam and to my family. Now I was divorced from my husband and sharing part-time custody of my children. Vietnam seemed like an apparition from the past. After my divorce, I became involved in an intense relationship with the director of the Bureau of Engraving and Printing of the US Treasury Department, Peter Daly. We had a crazy, torrid infatuation with each other, like out-of-control teenagers. Peter was a helpful mentor during those years when I was thrust into a mix of senior officials and high-net-worth individuals. He helped me appreciate my own worth and have confidence in my abilities. Our romantic relationship, however, proved too intense to survive.

Political Appointee: NJ Director of Historic Buildings

In 1996, New Jersey Governor Christine Todd Whitman appointed me as her state's director of historic buildings. My new housing was in Morven, the eighteenth-century former governor's mansion in Princeton. I began restoration on that residence and the New Jersey State House. Two years later, I returned to DC to work for the World Wildlife Fund, soliciting leadership gifts for their capital campaign focusing on gifts of $10 million and above. I followed that job with development officer positions at several other nonprofits.

Although I was deeply affected by my experiences in Vietnam, I focused on my current life—my children and work. Few people knew I had spent time in Vietnam. I wondered if Mai and my other Vietnamese friends were still alive.

CHAPTER 13

Searching for Mai

My children were now young adults; Nick was in college, and Maria Mai was employed in New York City. It seemed like the right time to make a trip to Vietnam. I had two hesitations. First, they would be traveling with "Mommy" and learning about Vietnam and the war solely through my lens. I didn't want to feel like a chaperone. I wanted the experience of a family trip even if we weren't the nuclear family we once were. The second hesitation—and the bigger one—is that I was clinging to the hope that I would locate Mai.

In the summer of 1999, David Bailey and Caroline Elliot invited me to her family's beach house in North Carolina. Our AFSC tenures in Vietnam overlapped for nearly two years, and I was grateful to join them that summer. One of the hardest parts of divorcing my husband was losing the partner with whom I had shared unique memories of Vietnam.

As we talked about our Vietnam days, I suggested a plan. Would they and their three adult children join me, Nick, and Maria Mai on a return trip? Caroline suggested we also invite Bob Redig and his wife. Coming from a farm family with strong Catholic roots, Bob had studied to become a priest, but ethical concerns about the church's position on the Vietnam War sidetracked him, and he volunteered to work for AFSC. Five young adults were on board with the plan, and we five older adults committed to the trip.

It was challenging, taking into account the complicated plans of ten people, several of whom arrived and left at different times. I organized the most important overlap time in Quảng Ngãi and managed travel from Hanoi to Saigon—now called Ho Chi Minh City—the length of the spine of Vietnam. It was incredible to be able to plan travel in northern Vietnam, US "enemy" territory for so many years.

Locating Mai

We didn't need a guide, but we wanted to hire a driver and small van to navigate the chickens, overloaded trucks, and other traffic clogging the main highway. I contacted an agent who had booked previous trips for AFSC delegations. Linh Chi and her husband, Victor, had left a large agency to start their own. Our email correspondence began with a barrage of questions about an itinerary that included Hanoi, the imperial city of Hue, the ancient port city of Hoi An, Cham temples near Tam Ky, and Ho Chi Minh City. We also wanted to visit the former site of AFSC at Quảng Ngãi, as well as Qui Nhon, the new Rehabilitation Center location.

Linh Chi suggested I eliminate the stop in Quảng Ngãi. "It's in one of the poorest regions of the country and was devastated by the war. There's not much to see or do there." With that, I poured out the story of how four of us had spent the war years living and working in Quảng Ngãi, and revisiting this city was a major reason for this journey.

I told Linh Chi how I had postponed traveling to Vietnam for so long because I wanted to return only if I could find my friend Mai. Even now, I was sorry I was going back before having located her. Linh Chi suggested, "You could advertise on Missing & Found on television. People have used this program since the end of the war to find people." I explained that I didn't know Mai's real name or where she lived. Though television broadcasting began in Vietnam in 1966, I never saw a television set in Quảng Ngãi during the time I lived in Vietnam. I couldn't imagine a TV program helping me to find Mai.

Linh Chi was my daughter's age and, like other tech-savvy young people, didn't let my ignorance of Mai's real name stop her. Linh Chi called what had been the former AFSC Rehabilitation Center in Qui Nhon and asked to speak with any staff person who had been there when the Quakers were working in Vietnam. Incredibly, Linh Chi spoke to Anh My, a close friend of Mai's, who said Mai was living in Tam Ky and was reachable by phone. Years of mystery were resolved with a single call to the right person.

From that point, Linh Chi was part of a triangular communication. I sent emails to her, and she telephoned Mai. Our plans depended on what Linh Chi could arrange. We hoped that Mai would come to Quảng Ngãi on a particular date and meet us at a specific hotel at four o'clock. During these back-and-forths, Linh Chi dropped an unexpected announcement. "Mai will bring her daughter."

Before our reunion, there was one direct exchange of letters. Mai answered like this:

Dear Jane and beloved children Mai and Hung [Mai had given Nick a Vietnamese name]

I got your letter full of excitement, expectation, and nostalgia. You and David were two good wartime friends.

Our governments hated each other. But we have passed across the boundaries of hatred to arrive together as true friends in the spirit of those who love each other. This human love doesn't know distinctions of skin color or political line. At the beginning when I met you and David at the Quảng Ngãi Hospital, I boldly put forward my opinion to my leaders, the revolutionary government at the local level. With one mind, they gave me permission to contact and befriend you so as to understand the reason for Quaker Service in Vietnam.

That would also help the American people more fully understand our justifiable war and that Vietnam people wanted independence, freedom, and peace. Meeting you two, I was like a fish in a basket, a severely wounded girl, an enemy of the nationalist cause, entirely in their power. But my heart always trusted you as friends, as good people, reliable protection for me while our people purposely clashed with each other, tried to kill each other.

The war is now past. After April 30, 1975, I was enormously happy and just wished that you two could be here to share my joy that my country had peace. It was like a dream—my timeworn dream came true—my country had peace.

Now to meet you again after thirty years, my fondest wish has been granted: to meet you, your two children, but my heart is very sad not to meet David on this trip. To this day, there is still "why" in my heart. Why? David has not walked the whole road of life together with you to help unfortunate people like me, like so many other people in other lands at war. Truly I am very sad, sad to meet you and your two children but without David. Let me take this opportunity to send David my best wishes and ask him to write to me to let me know how he is doing. My heart and memory after thirty years are still imprinted in firm strokes by the kind American couple from so far away, my beloved friends.

I want your children to love you a lot—as my daughter loves me. She reserves her whole love for her mother who sacrificed so much to make her into a productive person. That is our source of comfort when we get old.

Now thirty years later, I still feel fulfilled because I knew you. You are an example for young people because you put everything into helping others, sharing the suffering and misfortunes of others and to reduce their hardships. You are a true blessing. I want that blessing to go on forever for the lives of you and your children.

In a separate note to Maria Mai and Nick, she wrote

You two children, Mai and Hung, I am a Vietnamese mother who had many misfortunes as a woman in wartime Vietnam. In spite of that, I am very happy because I have a child and because I will meet you three people, though from faraway America, I have not forgotten you. I hope you become talented people, feeling people who know how to love others the way you love your own selves, as David and Jane loved me.

Arriving in Vietnam

I recognized the distinctive scent of Vietnam the minute we landed: the ubiquitous fermented fish sauce used in cooking, blended with diesel fumes and the sweet smell of familiar flowers. The sights and sounds spoke of peace—an abundance of shops and women carrying dual baskets on poles, balancing food and flowers for sale. Does peace have a sound? Yes. It is the absence of the sounds of war. I took deep breaths and slid into my return to Vietnam with hope and excitement.

One of the first items on the agenda was to meet with Linh Chi and Victor. No American travel agent had ever invited me to sit on the floor and enjoy a meal, but that is what happened at their house. Victor's parents (married women usually live with their in-laws) joined us. A plastic tablecloth was spread on the floor, and many separate dishes were arranged in the center. We sat, shoeless. In Vietnam, eating is a communal experience, emphasizing the importance of kinship, respect, and reverence for family. At home I served individual portions on separate plates; here we each shared the food before us. Sometimes Victor's mother would take a portion and put it in my bowl. "Here. Welcome. Let me share some food with you."

In the days before our children arrived, David Bailey, Caroline Elliot, and I traveled by train to the northern part of Vietnam, where we visited a rural market on the monthly market day. Here, near the Chinese border, female tribe members wore wax-resist, natural indigo-dyed textiles. Miniature horses, an exclusive breed to the area, trotted along paths carrying goods to and from the market, up the steep mountain paths. Several farmers rode their horses without saddles.

Lush hillsides were terraced with rice, their color as green as the skin of fresh limes. We trekked into the mountains along trails that took us into forests and open spaces. People were hard at work everywhere. Children stared at us in a curious but pleasant way, so unlike those who taunted us with "Mr. America, Mrs. America" during the war years. We were free to walk where we wanted without fear of stepping on American land mines. We didn't see any bomb craters.

Nick and Maria Mai arrived a day earlier in Hanoi than expected. When mapping out our calendar, I had forgotten about the international date line. They woke up the hotel owner at 1 a.m. Fortunately, the owner, a friend of a friend, found rooms for them, and everyone enjoyed teasing me over this error.

The next day, ten of us, with baggage, squeezed into a white van and began our adventure. We started with a relaxing overnight on Ha Long Bay, in the days before the tourist crush. It was as if we had stepped into a Chinese painting depicting limestone outcroppings rising from the ocean. It was surreal, this peaceful Vietnam.

We stopped to visit Cham temples in My Son, much smaller but similar to the Angkor Wat temple complex in Cambodia. Though the Cham people had migrated to Vietnam via maritime routes 5,000 years ago, I couldn't travel the mere fifteen miles from Quảng Ngãi to visit the temples during the war—at times the roads weren't secure due to fighting or the NLF controlled the area where the temples stood. Today they are an important tourist destination; however, when we visited, they weren't yet restored. We climbed among vines and overgrown vegetation and reflected on the complicated history of the Cham, who were driven out by the Viet people.

The road leaving the temples was full of potholes, and the van swerved and turned to avoid getting stuck in the mud or breaking an axle. My calculations of time were off. We were going to arrive in Quảng Ngãi later than the designated hour, and I was nervous.

In those pre-cell phone days, I had no way of reaching Mai as one hour grew to three hours late. When we arrived, I shoved the sliding door of the van open and rushed up the stairs into the hotel. A staff person answered my question. "Yes, there was an old woman waiting for you with another woman, but they left." I was frantic. I had come halfway around the world after thirty-five years and was convinced I had blown the chance to see Mai. Calling out to my daughter, I said, "Let's search around the hotel and neighborhood. Maybe they are resting somewhere." No luck.

I was hot, tired, and upset. But, as we turned a corner to come back, we saw Mai and Thuy on a small Honda motorbike. I recognized Mai immediately. She had short hair, cut just below the ears. Mine was no longer shoulder-length either, and the humidity had turned it into a curly halo. As Mai slid off the motorbike, we embraced. We hugged and hugged. Normally I would have been careful—a double amputee needs to use a crutch for balance—but, in this instance, I was holding so tight, we were like one tree that couldn't fall over. Our daughters stood watching. We finally let go, our faces wet with tears. "Mai," I said, "this is my daughter, Maria Mai. And this must be your daughter."

The two young women, the same age, shyly hugged. Thuy was as beautiful as her mother at that age, with long black hair pulled tightly off her face and held with an elastic band. Her hair fell down her back in a wide, loose braid. She wore tiny pearl earrings. My daughter was nearly a head taller than Thuy. Maria Mai's shoulder-length blond hair framed her long face and blue eyes. As was popular at the time, she wore several rings, one of which was a whimsical, red plastic blob, a funky look compared to the conventional way Vietnamese dressed. Mai grabbed my arm and shook it. "What? Is her name really Mai?" she asked.

"Yes," I replied, "I named her in honor of you, and this is the happiest moment for me—that Mai and Mai meet." That tickled Mai. There were more tears and laughter as the other familiar AFSC team members crowded around to say hello.

Mai and Jane reuniting in 2002

We were exhausted from sheer emotion. We ordered our favorite dishes in the hotel dining room and toasted Mai over and over. The hotel staff were curious. "How do you know these Americans?" they asked Mai. Other guests stared at this odd American group toasting two Vietnamese women.

Returning to Quảng Ngãi

The next morning, our group ventured out to explore Quảng Ngãi. The five former AFSC staffers searched for landmarks, but it was a changed city. After the war, the Vietnamese burst into action, clearing and rebuilding with frenzied energy. Many single-story buildings were replaced with two-story structures. New trees were planted, and front yards were decorated with urns containing colorful plants. In the center of town, we took Phan Boi Chau Street to locate the former AFSC Rehabilitation Center. As we approached the provincial hospital gate, a man leaning at a guard booth seemed to recognize us and asked if we were those Americans who made legs during the war. He proudly raised his pant leg and showed us his below-knee artificial leg. Mai laughed and, tapping with her cane, signaled him to come closer to look at her legs. She was delighted that her daughter was witnessing the fruits of her work for AFSC. My daughter and son, too, were beginning to learn about my war work.

Inside the hospital, a new iteration of the AFSC Center had been incorporated as a rehabilitation wing. The structure was still simple, with plain walls, but the roof was solid wood instead of tin. We wandered, disoriented. There were actual weights for the patients, not cement-filled tomato sauce or soup cans. Exercise tables had real mattresses, replacing straw mats.

Caroline and Mai were most interested in the physical therapy rooms. Caroline had been Mai's therapist, giving her muscle-strengthening exercises and having her practice walking between parallel bars until she could do it on her own. Mai's biggest trial had been overcoming her fear of climbing stairs, but with Caroline's encouragement, she became a functional double amputee. As they wandered around the room, they noticed something in the corner. Caroline let out a squeal. The old practice stairs Mai used thirty-five years ago were still there. At the time, rehab workers crafted these almost crude, wooden steps with a single handrail. Mai reminded Caroline of how terrifying it had been to practice. "It was like walking up stairs on stilts."

Those rudimentary stairs were also a reminder of my shock, when I first arrived in Vietnam, at the stark difference between the quality and quantity of goods in the US and similar items available here. However, I reflected on how, within months of my arrival, I had already begun to overlook the differences in substance to appreciate that the real separation between Vietnam and America was not the availability of material goods. The major difference lay in the spirit of the people.

There was little self-pity in Vietnam. I'd read stories about the anger and hopelessness of disabled Vietnam veterans in the US. Here, I observed determined people without limbs practicing with prosthetic legs. They looked forward to rejoining their villages, finding new ways to accommodate their disabilities and contribute to society. There was a profound sense of Buddhist acceptance combined with a drive to move forward. It was humbling.

Peace Trees and My Lai

Leaving the hospital, we crossed the Tra Kuc River toward My Lai. Thirty-five years ago, it would have been a familiar scene to watch two people, standing on the edge of a canal, each holding a thin rope attached to either side of a cone-shaped straw basket, rhythmically pulling water from the river. I once bought an irrigation basket to give as a wedding gift to a Vietnamese couple. There was a saying that it took two people in harmony to operate the basket; the task couldn't be done singlehandedly. Now irrigation was done mechanically. And the bridge wasn't in danger of being shelled. It was a hot, bumpy ride. We arranged to meet our contact at My Lai, a local man who had purchased young, healthy trees for us to plant with funds we'd raised from friends and family. The trees would be planted at the My Lai Peace Park, a project of Mike Boehm, a Vietnam veteran who came, year after year, to play his violin at My Lai. His tribute was a homegrown, one-man operation to soothe the spirits of villagers murdered at My Lai. Planting trees in their memory was part of Mike's project.

Mike had been deeply affected by the war. Working on the tree project and helping villagers with microloans was a way for Mike to heal and provide a meaningful vehicle for his trauma. For us, digging in the dirt and planting trees—ten people from two generations—was a simple act, but it was full of meaning and hope. For Nick and Maria Mai, it was an opportunity for questions. Mai sat in the shade and watched. She told me later that watching us, holding our shovels and working with our hands in the dirt, reminded her of her time as a teacher.

Bob Redig and Caroline Elliot planting Peace Trees at My Lai Peace Park

"When I was teaching at the Nguyen Van Troi School, the students and I had to work during the day to grow our own food, and then I taught them at night. If we didn't grow our own food, we would not eat. Some local farmers remained on the land even though it was a free fire zone. They lent us tools, like the hoe that Maria Mai is holding."

We had a cool drink after planting, and Mai gave Nick a *bo doi* hat, in soft fabric, with a narrow brim, worn by most of the NLF cadre. When I was first in Vietnam, I didn't know the significance of this style. Mai became a POW in part because she was wearing a *bo doi* when she was injured.

The Vietnamese have a deep sense of history in a way that Americans, living in a young nation, do not. Mai was thoughtful about our tree planting. She told the young adults in our group, "You have dug in the earth of Vietnam, and you understand the love we've had for our country for three thousand years. We started with the Chinese, then the Japanese, French, and Americans. Other nations wanted our land. We Vietnamese spilled our blood and sacrificed for the sake of keeping our ancestral lands for ourselves."

For the young people, the concept of thinking back thousands of years was impossible. They expressed their amazement to Mai. "We barely know the history of our grandparents, let alone any family or country history before that."

Next was a visit to an elementary school built with funds raised by Mike Boehm and Quakers in Madison, Wisconsin. Marge Nelson, an AFSC doctor, had come twice in recent years to teach fifth-grade English. The principal welcomed us with the courtesy and formality Vietnamese offer guests, and we were invited to visit an English class to ask questions. Some of the students were shy and giggled. Others raised their hands and wiggled with excitement while a few tentatively tried to catch our attention. Their questions were simple: "How old are you? When did you come to Vietnam? Do you like our country?" Then, the teacher suggested, "Why don't you elders explain to the students why you worked in Vietnam," and then, turning to the young members of our group, said, "You young people, tell us why you are in My Lai planting trees." The best Vietnamese speaker of our group, David Bailey, spoke to the students for a few minutes. They listened attentively. Then Mai took the floor. She didn't stand, but she didn't have to. Mai went into what I call "her public relations spiel." Though David comes from a long line of Quakers, Mai can be even more articulate in speaking about them. Mai described the Quaker mission and work in Vietnam.

Then Mai shared how the young people in our group had raised money for planting trees at the Peace Park and had come to Vietnam to foster reconciliation. Mai was serious describing AFSC's work during the war, although she added humor as she talked about how two of the young men, Rob and Nick, bought a bottle of snake wine to take back to the US, eliciting "oohs" and squeals from the students.

Mai also spoke about school and education during the war.

> You are the precious future of our country. When I was a teacher in the NLF areas, it was incredibly dangerous to

go to school. The pupils used baskets as desks in case we had to evacuate an area, leaving no trace that a school had been there. In 1966, when I was teaching, the Americans dropped bombs on us and killed eleven of my pupils who didn't reach the shelter in time. They were sacrificed for you to have this opportunity to live and study in peace. Those students were obedient and disciplined. Let them be your models.

Fifty pupils, twenty-five in each class, grades five and six. When the planes bombed, we jumped into our tunnels. I often fled the bombing with another young male teacher who was a close friend. It was a scary time, but I recall how we laughed when we jumped into a tunnel with fire ants. They were biting us like crazy. We couldn't move in the tunnel, and we didn't dare climb out. I said, "Bomb us, Americans, and take us out of our misery. Of course, I didn't really mean that."

Mai ended with a reminder.

When I was teaching the pupils from farming families, they were of all ages, even though they were at the fifth and sixth levels. Some were almost as big as me. Later, they went on to be soldiers, becoming even high-ranking officers, and every year on November 20, Teacher's Appreciation Day, I get gifts from some of them. Be grateful to your teachers and study well.

At recess, in the courtyard, we were surrounded by children who spoke over each other as they asked questions. Maria Mai and Nick, who have a particular affinity for younger children, were enchanted. Like Vietnamese women, children also hold hands. Some hugged each other while they spoke to us. Perhaps this made them feel more comfortable while speaking English with these tall, young American strangers. One of my all-time favorite photos is of two schoolboys, one with his arm around the other's shoulder, while they spoke to my son.

Students from My Lai Elementary School with Nicholas and Maria Mai Barton

We left the school to visit a small museum at My Lai[44], where the names and ages of people killed there were listed. The photographs were covered with plastic film that was buckled and stained. Having worked at the National Gallery of Art in the US, with expensive displays designed by graphic artists and exhibition specialists, the museum was surprisingly modest. In recent years, as more tourists and students have flocked to Vietnam, it has been significantly upgraded.

The exhibits depicted the brutality of American soldiers who killed more than 500 women and children. The text and photographs included the story of US pilot Hugh Thompson and his two crewmen, who landed their helicopter between advancing American troops and the Vietnamese civilians the soldiers intended to kill. The crew threatened to kill fellow soldiers if they came any closer. This action saved the lives of some of the Vietnamese villagers.

We went to Buddha Mountain, overlooking the My Lai village area, with a pagoda attended by a few monks. This small mountain was our retreat during the war years. We needed to decompress and sit in the shade of an old banyan tree. My son, Nick, immediately forged a nonverbal relationship with Mai. He was solicitous, quietly helping

---

44 PBS, American Experience, Vietnam War, transcript, Interview: Larry Colburn

her in and out of the van. Later in college, he spoke of her when assigned a presentation on "one of the most important people I've met in my life." Nick talked about how two women, with different religious backgrounds and levels of education, had become friends despite their countries being at war.

There were memorable conversations on the mountain. The young adults were troubled by their day at My Lai. We, of course, knew the story. But the young people were full of questions—hard questions about the brutality of US troops and the years of lies and cover-ups. I was grateful Bob Redig was with us. His working-class roots gave some insight into the mind and actions of the young men who did the killing—how disoriented they were in a strange land where the enemy seemed to evaporate. The museum doesn't highlight this, but I told them, "You will hear many views on the massacre. Remember one simple fact that will help you know the massacre cannot be excused or justified: 125 children under the age of five were killed."

I had known someone who escaped the massacre. Ba Toi was twenty-four. She had gone to get banana leaves near her house and was raped by a soldier when she came back. Toi's mother, sisters, oldest brother, two youngest brothers, and an uncle were murdered. Months later, when the surviving villagers were forced by ARVN soldiers to build their own refugee camp, Toi stepped on a mine, losing all four limbs. She received two artificial arms and two legs at the AFSC Center. I remember her trying to walk between the parallel bars. She had a hard time gripping the bars to balance, but she was strong.

After the enormous effort of learning to walk and use her natural-looking prosthetic arm and a hook-device, Toi accepted a microloan from AFSC to open a tiny concession stand selling canned milk, tobacco, and cooking supplies. I took a photo of her—her front teeth missing from the mine explosion—standing tall, with arms extending out to each side to show off her prosthetic limbs. In 1973, after the Peace Accords were signed and all warring parties agreed to a cease fire, Toi was killed by an ARVN plane bombing My Lai.

Ba Toi, survivor of My Lai massacre and quadruple amputee with one "hook" arm and the other— Quy's hand invention

It was important for those of us who had worked for AFSC in Vietnam to share our individual memories with these young adults. I wanted my children to learn about my life in Vietnam, not just my war stories.

The day left us exhausted, but I had one last tale. "When helicopter pilot Thompson returned to Vietnam, he met some of the villagers whose lives he had saved. One woman asked, 'Why didn't the people who committed those acts come back with you?' At first, Thompson was taken aback by her remarks, but she went on to finish her sentence, 'so that we could forgive them.'"

The war was long over, and there we were, two generations gathered to reflect and enjoy the peace of this place. The Vietnamese are building their future.

Leaving Mai

Our itinerary was complicated, and our time was too short. I had days of questions for Mai. Where was her husband? What was her role during the war when she was living in the liberated territories? What happened to "Uncle Nam," the NLF officer? I was rarely alone with Mai and had no chance to explain why David hadn't walked down the road of life with me. She didn't know we came to Vietnam partly to heal our marriage—and that healing didn't happen. We stayed together to follow through on our mission to the Vietnamese people—to help stop the war. My memories of Vietnam were interwoven with David, but by the time Mai and I reunited, David and I had gone our separate ways.

Mai had overcome obstacles and trauma. She was strong, still had her wry humor and a delightful laugh. Her lovely, talented daughter, Thuy, admired her mother, and the two were close.

Other team members wanted to talk to Mai too, and the young adults were fascinated by her stories. I wanted to be selfish and American—"I want my answers now"—but remembered, in Vietnam, truth sometimes unrolls slowly. I would come back to find out more of Mai's story, what she was doing on the day her legs were blown off, how her beautiful daughter had come into the world.

Later, I wrote to her.

> *I had so many questions. I wish you could tell me the story of your life. What were you like as a little girl? How many siblings did you have, and were they involved in the revolution? What was your life like before we met? . . . You are my best friend, and yet there is much I still don't know about you. When we lived together in Quảng Ngãi, you could not tell me about yourself until you trusted me, and once you trusted me, our time flew by. I can't wait to see you again.*

We traveled to Qui Nhon to visit the new Rehabilition Center. It was utterly amazing to see the former Vietnamese trainees and Quy and Mỹ running the place. A planted seed grew into a full, independent tree now.

CHAPTER 14

Revolutionary Women
Tam Ky and Quảng Ngãi

I was eager to return to Vietnam. In 2005, while living in Washington, DC, I secured a grant from the William Joiner Institute for the Study of War and Social Consequences at the University of Massachusetts.[45] It allowed me and a former AFSC Vietnam colleague, Sophie Quinn-Judge, to interview women who had been active in the war effort. Sophie was an assistant professor of Vietnamese Studies at Temple University, having received her PhD from the prestigious School of Oriental and African Studies in London. Her books, *Ho Chi Minh: The Missing Years* and *The Third Force in the Vietnam War*, made influential contributions to the history of Vietnam.

The grant proposal included interviewing Mai and other women who had worked for the National Liberation Front in South Vietnam. Films and photographs produced by the North Vietnamese illustrated the patriotism of North Vietnamese women in the struggle against the American aggressor. However, women in South Vietnam who took part in the independence movement—the NLF—rarely, if ever, had their stories recorded, individually or collectively.

As time grew closer for my second return to Vietnam, I was filled with anticipation at seeing Mai and knowing that I would be immersing myself in the sights and sounds of Vietnam again. Sophie

---

45   We received a small grant from the Rockefeller Foundation through the William Joiner Institute.

and I traveled to Tam Ky, in central Vietnam, before launching into the project interviews, to be conducted in Quảng Ngãi and Danang. When Mai learned Sophie and I would be coming to visit her, she wrote a happy letter:

> *Today I am preparing for the New Year's celebration; in five days it will be Tet. Do you remember how, in 1972, we all went to visit Anh Bich in Duc Pho?*[46] *Our Vietnamese Tet is very joyful, lots of flowers are displayed throughout the house, the ancestral altar is on the table, and everybody puts on new clothing, new sandals, everything new. On the streets, the motorbikes whizz by; inside [the house] there are sweet cakes, fruits to welcome the ancestors back for Tet. We are careful to keep the traditions of the past.*
>
> *I am reading your letter where you say . . . you and Sophie will be making a trip back to Vietnam. Once you are here, call my phone. My house has three telephone numbers because I run a postal office branch in my home. If one number is busy, just try another. I will come get you to bring you back to my little place. We'll have lots of fun, talk, and then go to the Phu Ninh Reservoir. Oh, it will be fun.*

Visiting Mai in Tam Ky was remarkable. There was enough time to laugh and talk, see her home, and meet members of her circle: Thuy's husband, Long (pronounced "Lom"), their baby, and Thuy's in-laws. We skipped tourist spots and instead traveled to stay in Mai's house and eat home cooking. Sophie and I arrived by taxi to Mai's address and found her standing proudly in front of her house, as if it were a common practice for her to welcome American friends. I gave Mai a tight, strong hug.

I was impressed with the way Mai had set herself up to live

---

46   Many patients at the Rehabilitation Center came from Duc Pho, a heavily fought-over area during the war. Duc Pho is also the place where diarist Dang Thuy Tram had her underground hospital and where she was killed by US soldiers.

independently. While Thuy was in Saigon studying at the University of Saigon, Mai invited two nieces to live with her. They helped with chores, and Mai provided free lodging while they attended nursing school. Mai was enormously proud of Thuy for being accepted at the university and graduating four years later, though they could only see each other twice a year. After graduation, Thuy returned to Tam Ky to live with Mai until she married. She was living with her in-laws not far from Mai's house.

Mai lived in a shotgun-style house, common in most Vietnamese cities. The façade was one-room wide and open to the street. At night a metal accordion gate was drawn across the opening for privacy and security. Strips of colored plastic hung across a section of the open front. Two steps separated the house from the sidewalk. The bustle of street life was close.

The rooms were connected, one after the other—the living room, followed by an open dining area, then a bedroom with a door, and, finally, a Western-style bathroom. A passageway ran along the right side of the house, from the living room to a kitchen in the back. It was open to the sky, with a metal, corrugated roof over one section. The tiled floor was sloped toward a drain in the middle of the room for easy cleaning. In one corner, a hose attachment could be used to wash vegetables or take a shower. There was no stove or washing machine. The house was simple and functional.

Mai's home was attached to another house on the right. To the left, a narrow space—a path—separated Mai's house from the next, serving as a sidewalk behind the block-long row of houses. While I was in the bedroom, a face might bob two feet from the window or a vendor might call out to sell some food. The small windows in Mai's house had security bars, but it was too hot to hang curtains, since every breeze needed to be allowed into the house, even if that meant not a lot of privacy. Sophie and I chatted with Mai, drank tea, and began to relax.

Mai was eager to explain how she lived.

I am lucky to receive a small monthly disability allowance from the government, but it is not enough to cover my expenses. So, I set up a small business in the front room of my house to supplement my income. I operate a satellite post office and receive a tiny percentage of the cost of phone calls made when I connect a customer to a desired number; I sell stamps too. See those phone booths right here in my living room? I sit behind this small table with drawers and take telephone orders and sell stamps. When a customer gives me a phone number, I direct the customer to one of the booths, where, as the telephone operator, I connect the customer to the number he wants to call. It would have been fun if we'd had telephone service when I was fighting in the jungle. Messages came mostly by foot.

After a simple meal, we settled in. There wasn't much business in Tam Ky in the evening. Nevertheless, our nightly conversations were occasionally interrupted by someone wanting to make a call. When that happened, Mai made the transaction quickly, connecting the switchboard and the phone booth, and taking payment when the customer finished. It barely paused our conversation. Three years later, when I returned to Vietnam, the entire population was using cell phones for pleasure and business, including Mai.

Mai was anxious for me to visit with Thuy, meet Mai's baby granddaughter, and get to know Thuy's in-laws. "First, let's just have girl time and talk," Mai said. And we did. We talked and talked. Finally, Mai offered Sophie and me her bed. "Where are you sleeping, Mai, if you give us your bed?" I asked. Mai laughed. "Don't worry about me. I will sleep on the kitchen chopping block table. I'll just put a mat over it. When I take off my legs, I am the size of the table." Mai always seemed to find a solution. Sophie and I slept on Mai's platform bed on a woven plastic mat about one-eighth of an inch thick. The mat was intended to create a buffer between our bodies and the hard, wooden bed.

The next day, Mai phoned Thuy, who soon arrived on her motor scooter. Thuy took the stage when I asked about her work. She was employed at a television station, but I knew little more than that. Mai's pride was obvious as Thuy told us her story.

I majored in journalism, and I really wanted to get into working at a newspaper or television station. Now that the war was over, the country needed a whole new crop of journalists. People try to say the Communists have a Party line, but now people demand timely and in-depth news stories. I am an anchor on the prime-time news station. Rather than read a script researched and written by someone else, the way I understand it is done in America and Europe, I am required to conduct my own research and prepare the news story. Recently I've begun to take more of a producer role, and last month, I was even sent to another section of the country with a film crew to produce a small news piece.

When I first secured my position, there was a little grumbling that I had a slight advantage over other candidates whose family had sided with the Americans and South Vietnamese government. My mother is a Communist Party member and a wounded veteran, but I don't think I was given favoritism. In any case, it didn't take me long to prove to the whole staff that I was deserving of being hired. It's unfortunate that some people think there is prejudice because of the past. The war ended so long ago. We have to unite to create our new society.

Thuy wore modest, unadorned clothes and had a quiet demeanor. She giggled when her television producers insisted she wear a nice *au dias* (traditional Vietnamese dress) and lipstick while being filmed.

Like her mother, Thuy had inner fortitude, and I knew she appeared on television as a dignified, poised, and beautiful woman delivering major news stories.

Thuy also filled us in on the birth of her little girl, An Khue.

I am proud that I didn't have to participate in the old draconian Vietnamese mores surrounding the birth of a baby and the treatment of the mother. Many families still insist that new mothers not wash their hair or shower for months after a birth because hot or cold showers might upset the delicate balance between hot and cold qualities that are essential in the body. Only sponge baths are allowed.

Mai's daughter Thuy, her husband and daughter

I told Mai I remembered patients at the Rehabilitation Center talking of "hot and cold winds" in their bodies and how it had taken me a while to interpret the medical significance. Mai took a contemporary outlook on childbirth. "I think some of the traditional practices for pregnant women are ridiculous and even unhealthy," she said.

Thuy agreed, noting that some women follow a practice called "mother roasting."

The poor mother sits by a heat source and sweats. Then there are all these dietary restrictions—eat this, don't eat that, cold soup will cause you to bleed, hot peppers can make your milk stop. I'm grateful that my mother is enlightened and not old-fashioned. I was able to have a modern birth and go back to work. At the same time, it was fun and cozy for me and the baby to be together with my mother at her house after the birth. We were happy to be together like the days before I married.

As she readied to leave, Thuy invited us to see An Khue and meet Thuy's in-laws. "We'll go on a boat ride on the new man-made lake, Phu-Ninh Reservoir, up toward the mountains," Thuy said. "It will be a very pleasant outing."

Meeting the in-laws was daunting. Their house was larger and more gracious than Mai's, with separate rooms and a courtyard and a small piece of land with flowers and trees sheltering it from the street. Thuy's father-in-law sat on a couch in full military regalia, a green uniform and rows of medals. According to Thuy, he was an important general in the North Vietnamese Army, and he wanted us to know that. He had gone North in 1954 but, when the war ended, came back to his hometown, Tam Ky. The reason was simple: Vietnamese are inexorably linked to their "que," or birthplace, because the tombs of their ancestors lay there. Thuy's mother-in-law, a Northerner by birth, had also been an officer in the army. She wore her hair in a short bob and had a gap between her front teeth. Her manner was friendly, though reserved. Her Northern accent was extremely difficult to understand, so she brought her face closer and spoke louder. Sophie and I smiled. We didn't converse a lot with the in-laws, using the excuse we couldn't wait to see the grandchild.

Khue was, of course, adorable, and Sophie and I gave her the gifts we brought. We played with her while she lay on a bed with a thin—but real—mattress. Long was able to get away from his engineering job at the Danang Harbor, where he worked on deepening the waterway to accommodate larger commercial ships. He has a tapered, slender face, and his eyes crinkle and nearly close when he smiles. His laugh is contagious.

It was lovely to see Thuy settled, although I picked up on an undercurrent that her in-laws expected her to perform traditional wifely duties, cooking and cleaning, even with the new baby and work. Thuy was not always finding it easy to deal with the many demands of her time.

The next day, we five women—Mai, Thuy, Thuy's mother-in-law, Sophie, and I—visited Lake Phu Ninh, which provides more water and electric power to the region. It sits in the middle of nowhere. We took a ride in a boat decorated with awnings and tassels in yellow and red, Vietnamese colors. I was impressed with how Mai had maintained her facility to walk with her prostheses. First she placed her right leg below-the-knee prosthesis out in front before moving her Canadian crutch parallel to that foot. Then she swung her left crutch and her above-the-knee leg forward, bearing down to lock the knee joint so she could put weight on it. It was slow going. Step by step.

Interviews with NLF Women

We began the process of interviewing women who had traveled to Quảng Ngãi to tell their stories. Sophie, Mai, and I had reached out to various sources to identify women who were willing to record their history. Some had worked with a female doctor, Dang Thuy Tram, whose published diary, *Last Night I Dreamed of Peace*, was a bestseller. In it, she describes a young soldier, whom she calls "little brother," who was, by then, a Communist Party official in Quảng Ngãi. He helped with logistics and ensured our schedule went smoothly. Though Sophie and I speak Vietnamese, we hired a translator, Thao, to ensure absolute accuracy to the notes we were taking in English. We also recorded each woman as she spoke Vietnamese.

We spent three days interviewing ten women who had worked for the NLF. Most interviews lasted two hours. They ranged in age from fifty-seven to seventy and held varying levels of responsibility. These women came prepared and told their stories with dignity and pride. One woman wore a new blouse and matching pants made for the occasion, in addition to taking three long bus rides to reach Quảng Ngãi.

The women shared one thing in common: they came from families and regions with a nationalist tradition. Almost all their mothers and fathers, directly or indirectly, were active against the French and Americans. Moreover, the opportunity to take an active role in the struggle for independence gave them a chance to be "their fathers' sons." Boys, by Confucian tradition, are more cherished than girls. When the war broke down rules, girls stepped into male roles and escaped many of the traditional restrictions on women in their society.

The stories of a few cannot adequately reflect the broad range of women drawn into the ranks of the NLF. In Quảng Ngãi, we interviewed women who mostly fought at a local level. Later, in Danang, we interviewed two who represented the NLF/PRG in several international countries. Some US military had no concept of the importance of South Vietnamese women, whom they thought of as second-class citizens, only capable of prostitution and service work on military bases. This superior attitude ironically helped the Vietnamese war effort, as the women could sometimes operate on behalf of the Viet Cong right under the noses of the US military. An AFSC team member watched US soldiers, examining the bags of the "hooch women," who cleaned the military dorms, as they left the base. The soldiers were checking to see if the women had stolen anything. My colleague began talking to one of the women in Vietnamese who remarked, "They should have been examining what is in our minds and memory, not what we might have in our bags."

Nguyen thi Cho as young soldier with her AK47 and soft brim hat; posing against backdrop in photo studio 2000

One loyal female cadre, Nguyen Thi Cho, was from Quảng Ngãi. Her mother, father, and brother were killed fighting the Americans. She directed a unit of thirty guerrillas. Cho brought a photograph of herself as a youth, looking like a ten-year-old Boy Scout, wearing a soft-brim hat with her ears sticking out, kneeling while holding her AK-47. Cho, herself, had killed at least three American soldiers.

Cho had another photograph, after the war ended, taken against a painted background of tulips and a waterfall. She is wearing a dazzling, reddish-orange *ao dia* with gold and stardust patterns swirling down the center, a jade bracelet, and a black purse with a gold tassel. What a contrast. The guerrilla fighter who related the story of running zigzag while dodging bullets in an escape—like an action shot from a movie—was this elegant woman posing before a fake backdrop.

Despite American propaganda that every Vietnamese fighting against the US and South Vietnamese militaries were Communists, the conclusion of the interviews was that few of these NLF women were actually members of the Communist Party. The women talked of years of rigorous self-examination and mentoring before they might be accepted into the Party, even on a probationary basis.

There was a powerful link among the women: the high personal cost of being part of the NLF. A few found meaningful employment, but others were on their own after the war, carrying heavy emotional and physical burdens. For example, Co, the Communist Party member who told diarist Dang Thuy Tram she wasn't ready to become a member, made huge sacrifices. She was separated from her husband for twenty-one years, during which he married someone else. Co lives in her village alone and poor.

Our interviews gave the women time to reflect and remember heroic moments in their youth. They expressed an enormous feeling of purpose, and none regretted their roles.

Mai's presence as a wounded NLF cadre member, and our friend, helped build trust during the interviews. She told the women of our work in Vietnam and how Sophie had been captured and released by the NLF in 1974. The women seemed to have no hesitation talking to us. We asked that they tell the simple truth. Thao was an excellent interpreter. Every night she, Sophie, and I went back to our hotel, ate together, and summarized the day. Mai was in her element and began to instruct Thao about the war. Teacher Mai was delighted to fill in the information a young person—born after the war ended—had missed, the details and rationale for what happened. Thao's father had fought for the NLF and been killed, but most of her knowledge of the war came from books. Her mother raised six daughters and didn't have time to explain the history, politics, and finer points of the conflict.

We returned to Tam Ky and left Mai at her home. Sophie, Thao, and I continued to Danang. We had become friends, the way women do after sharing an intense experience. Thao insisted we were "family" and encouraged us to stay at her mother's house during our two days of interviews. Sophie and I tried to beg off with the usual excuses of not wanting to be "in the way" or "troubling her mother," but we were grateful.

Morning was my favorite part of the day. We began with a bowl of *pho*, traditional Vietnamese soup. I'd hop on the back of Thao's scooter, and we'd go to some hole-in-the-wall restaurant specializing in beef *pho*. We'd select the cut of meat we wanted to add to the bone broth and noodles—tripe, oxtail, brisket, flank steak—grab a table, and wait for our deep bowls and plate of garnishes. Bottles of hot sauce and fish sauce were on every table. I liked the ceremony of preparing herbs to put in my bowl, breaking off part of a Thai basil stem before adding the leaves, dunking clumps of bean sprouts, squeezing a slice of lime, adding circles of cut, red chilis with fiery seeds, and flavoring the soup with more hot sauce or *nuoc mam*. It was an act of individualizing the *pho* to my taste. Yet, there was a communal aspect too. Sitting on miniature chairs with a crowd of people and relishing variations of the same type of soup was an experience unique to Vietnam.

Dinners were more complex. Thao's mother and youngest sister offered a mini banquet around a large piece of oilcloth with a lively pattern of red and pink flowers. In the center was an arrangement of different foods, colors, and textures. I regretted that Mai wasn't there.

Nguyen thi Kim Phuong with medals 1968; at home in Danang 2005

In Danang, Sophie and I conducted interviews with two women who had reached a level of national importance within the NLF. Nguyen Thi Kim Phuong was waiting for us in her gracious, cool house. Phuong's path took her to Cambodia, where, in the 1950s, she organized the Vietnamese expat community to support the revolution and coordinated shelter for Vietnamese escaping into Cambodia. In another phase of her life, during the '60s, she worked at the Central Office for South Vietnam (COSVN). The US military called COSVN the "Bamboo Pentagon." President Richard Nixon was obsessed with obliterating these headquarters, believing the destruction of the command post would cripple their power. In 1965, 400 B52s dropped bombs every day to wipe out the nonexistent Bamboo Pentagon. In reality, Phuong told us, COSVN was composed of many small mobile huts, which were frequently forced to move.

As part of her work, Phuong wrote training materials and directed a twenty-day training program for sixty women in Region Five, consisting of three provinces: Quảng Ngãi, where the AFSC project was located; Quang Nam, where Mai was born and operated with the NLF; and the neighboring province of Binh Dinh. Phuong had to move the women's training site three different times. When Phuong described the training, such as how to speak to ARVN soldiers to persuade them to defect, I was reminded of the language Mai used as a propaganda official. She would say, "Brothers, remember your families, your land. Why are you fighting for the foreigners? Come home and help make your country free." Perhaps Mai attended one of Phuong's programs. On the day Mai was injured, she had conducted a training program for women.

Phuong was working in North Vietnam when she met Ho Chi Minh in 1968. Later, she was head of the Women's Union in Region Five. In 1973 Phuong saw her children for the first time in fifteen years. She said her daughter was shy and withdrawn until she came to know her mother again. Today, Phuong and her husband are happily retired in Danang.

Phan thi Minh, former representative for Provincial Revolutionary Government (PRG) at the Paris Peace Talks, with her high school classmates at a French school in Vietnam; Minh walking in front of her house in 2005

Another interviewee was Phan thi Minh (birth name: Le thi Kinh). By the age of fifteen, she was organizing student protests against the French and then was imprisoned for three years. With time, she moved through a range of posts, including serving in Paris as a member of the negotiating team at the Paris Peace Talks. The French called her "Queen of the Viet Cong." At one point, US National Security Advisor Henry Kissinger accused Minh of stalling the talks; Minh said Kissinger was "vain." As visitors, we entered her house through a photography shop, and as our taxi drove away, we saw Minh gently sweeping the sidewalk.

The following day, Mai arrived in Danang in a hired car. Mai, Sophie, and I said goodbye to Thao and her family and boarded the flight to Hanoi. After interviewing women who were part of the movement to create an independent Vietnam, I was now turning to the NLF woman I knew best. I longed to know Mai's story.

We placed Mai's wheelchair in the trunk of the taxi. I knew she was going to enjoy her first plane ride, and indeed, she smiled and chatted as we wheeled around the airport. The staff was courteous to Mai, and I wondered if any of these young people had met war veterans without legs. Mai and her wheelchair were raised to the plane door on a forklift. I was sorry I didn't have a photo of her waving from her perch in the air. She enjoyed the hour-and-a-half flight, looking at the earth and clouds from above.

CHAPTER 15

Mai Reveals Her Secrets

Arriving in Hanoi was a historic moment for Mai. As a result of her family's anti-French, anti-American tradition and struggle, Mai, and relatives who died for the cause, had dreamed of a unified Vietnam and a celebratory trip to Hanoi. Finally, thirty years after the war, she was making the trip.

Hanoi: Setting

Sophie had arranged for us to stay in the house of a friend who was planning to be away. When we arrived at the Hanoi airport, Sophie went ahead in one cab, while Mai, the wheelchair, and I took another one. We tried to give the cab driver directions, and, finally, he asked, "Will you women please speak Vietnamese?" Mai retorted, "I am speaking Vietnamese. I am Vietnamese, and I fought to bring this country peace so the North and South could be united." The taxi driver apologized. "I'm sorry. I have never heard an accent like yours." *Ah yes*, I thought, *a silent reminder not to be surprised by Northerners who think their accent is more correct than that of the central coast.*

Like many areas in Vietnam, houses in Hanoi were built over centuries, adding sections higgledy-piggledy, creating alleyways that twisted and turned. I loved walking these alleys, peeking over gates into courtyards, and seeing people with their families and birds singing in bamboo cages. The cab driver maneuvered off the main road and through the maze, getting close enough for Mai to walk to the house, a three-story dwelling with a garden in front and a lovely, wooden doorway. Inside, the tile floor led through a small kitchen to a living room from which we could see a garden of ceramic containers filled with flowers. On one wall of the living room hung a substantial, contemporary painting of a Buddha with a gold leaf background. Stairs leading to the second and third floors were made of exotic dark wood.

Sophie and I took rooms upstairs, and Mai had a sofa bed and bath on the first floor. From an open terrace, I could see Hanoi's landmark West Lake and the extensive buildings and development surrounding it. This view marked another stage in Vietnam's recovery from the war. The bombed-out Bach Mai Hospital had been rebuilt, and bomb shelter holes, once lining the streets, were gone. Bikes were replaced by motorcycles, cars, and even large tourist buses. Vietnam was modernizing fast.

The house was as luxurious as any I had visited in the US, but Mai didn't say anything about being impressed. In fact, it took a day or two for us to get comfortable in the house. We took time to be tourists. It had been Mai's dream to see North Vietnam. Unification was the goal of the independence movement, and she wanted to see "the other side of her heart," as she called it. Mai had hoped to be invited to see it, be chosen for a training program, or continue her education in the north. That didn't happen. Instead, her first visit to Hanoi was with us, her American friends.

Ho Chi Minh's Mausoleum

My favorite stop in Hanoi was Ho Chi Minh's mausoleum because it was so meaningful to Mai. When a guard saw Mai in her wheelchair, we were ushered to the front of the line. To our consternation, the only access to the entrance was up a long, white marble staircase. But soon, two guards picked up the chair and carried Mai like an empress in a palanquin. My eyes teared up. Mai may have been overlooked in the postwar years, but she had managed to create a great life for herself despite her handicaps. She was a queen and deserved to be carried to meet "Uncle Ho."

The guards brought her down the stairs, and the three of us posed for a picture when we reached the plaza. In former decades, some Vietnamese were afraid of having their photo taken in case the camera captured their spirit and took it away. If they allowed it, they wanted to look formal and dignified and requested copies of portraits to place on an ancestral altar after they died. Mai was usually comfortable, and I have many photos of her generous smile. However, she wore a somber expression. Afterwards, Mai said, "Uncle Ho and I are going to have a conversation about wheelchair accessibility to his tomb." She laughed even as her eyes filled with tears.

Mai's Life

Over the next few days, Sophie and I sat in the living room of our temporary home, with a tape recorder and notebooks, as Mai began to tell her story of life with the NLF and personal secrets she had kept locked inside. Vietnamese have a long view of time, and Mai seemed to be content having waited three decades to reveal these secrets while I—an impatient American—wanted to learn them immediately. Listening to Mai was emotionally draining, and I could tell it was far more stressful for her. She said, "Sophie, we didn't know each other as well because you worked in the AFSC Saigon office, but now we are sharing our lives together." After two hours, Mai suggested we take a break. "The next part of my life is a happy one," she said. "I got new legs and became a close friend with you, Jane."

Mai invited her sister-in-law, Dao, who lived in Hanoi, to join us for tea the next day. Dao had done graduate work in Australia, spoke excellent English, and described her work with the UN as an agricultural consultant. She had traveled internationally, and her children were close to their cousins, Mai's grandchildren. Mai's daughter had married into an educated family with an esteemed military service background.

After Dao's visit, we went to the Temple of Literature. The temple is surrounded by a great wall with a central gate and spans five courtyards. It was easy to push Mai's wheelchair along the walkways. Vietnam's first university was established there in 1076, six years after the temple was founded.

Mai and I were serious when we spoke about the causes of the war. But we shook our heads over the fact that Americans came to Vietnam referring to the people as "gooks" and hadn't bothered to study their history. The brilliant military minds of the Vietnamese had defeated the French and were going to defeat them too. Mai also added, "Our poetry helped keep us alive. A little poetry might have been good for the GIs. They were even further away from home than us. At least this was our own land we were fighting for."

We stopped at a sidewalk restaurant, where we found a full-size chair for Mai rather than the customary miniature stools. We spent a bit more time sightseeing, and then Mai announced she was ready to resume her story.

Mai's Affair

Are you tired, Jane and Sophie? Should I go on? The next part is a precious chapter in my life. I was convinced I was capable of having a child.

In December 1975, just two months after the confrontation with Ly, I was pregnant! Can you believe it? Now of course you are dying to know who was the father of my baby Thuy, eh? [Mai chuckled.] Well, it was pretty amazing and romantic. I met a young and extremely handsome—if I do say so myself—high school teacher named Tuan who was studying in Quảng Ngãi. He was a decade younger than me, and I was very much in love with him.

What I liked best was the way he would stroke my stumps and tell me how they were heroic symbols of my sacrifice for the revolution. He adored these. [Mai touched her stumps as she made this declaration.] He called them sexy. He knew how to touch me so that I would moan with love. I was happy. I was also breaking taboos. An older woman having a child with a man over ten years younger than she. A "maimed" woman with a "whole" man. A married woman bearing the child of a very eligible single man, the oldest son in this family.

Mai looked at us, realizing the intensity of her emotions and the effect on us. Sophie and I were reeling, trying to merge the new pieces of the story with the Mai we had come to know in Quảng Ngãi in the 1970s.

Mai told us she felt sexually attractive despite being disabled. This was a salient moment for me, after my crisis following evacuation orders in Quảng Ngãi, when I was fearful of losing my legs, of not being able to ski or wear heels or feel sexy. I was humbled and ashamed of myself, but I didn't dwell on this epiphany. I was concentrating on Mai. She had never shared these thoughts, but they shaped my thinking going forward.

Pregnant with Thuy and Seeking Communist Party Permission

I hadn't planned on getting pregnant so quickly or with such a man as Tuan. Now my greatest hurdle was to secure the permission of the Communist Party to have a child out of wedlock. Since the liberation, the Party wanted its members to set the highest ethical and work standards as an example to the new population of South Vietnamese who were watching us as role models. Single women in the Party were warned against becoming pregnant. Personally, at that time, I felt that the Party taking an uncompromising stance against single mothers was in direct conflict with the many women who had delayed marriage to devote themselves to the war effort, and now they couldn't find husbands due to the large numbers of males killed in both the north and the south. These women, like me, wanted a partial family and needed someone to care for them in their old age.

I knew of another single woman who had asked to have a child. The Party put her through an intense month of criticism. My friend became desolate and depressed. She had already given up the younger years of her life, and now the Party was placing a burden on her. She knew she would never marry, but it was hard to give up the dream of having a child. With this example in mind, I went directly to the Party Secretary of my region and presented him with my dilemma. I said to him, 'I have no legs, and I'm getting older. I have met a single man who is willing to have a child with me, a child that will help her mother in her old age. I am now pregnant with that child, and I want to keep it and give birth.' This was a lot to say to a higher official, but I felt strongly about my position and about the baby in my tummy. The secretary seemed startled and hesitated. 'I'll give it consideration,' he said.

Just five days later, the secretary got back to me. He suggested I raise the issue with members of my Communist cell and tell them that he had given me the green light to proceed. I knew the major reason he made the exception for me was that I was a wounded veteran. How about that? What an irony. I lose my legs and need a child to take care of me; I am allowed to have a child because I have lost my legs. On May 8, 1976, I gave birth to a perfect baby girl and named her Thuy. It was one of the happiest days of my life.

Around the time of Thuy's birth, the Rehabilitation Center was moved to Qui Nhon, about a hundred miles south. The relocation was fortuitous for Mai, at least at first.

Move to Qui Nhon—and Tuan Seeks Permission to Marry

Tuan, Thuy's father, had accepted a job to teach at the local Qui Nhon high school, and we lived together for seven months. It was a wonderful opportunity. Tuan was proud of Thuy, and he loved being affectionate with his daughter. Whenever he tickled Thuy, she'd giggle until she got the hiccups. But within the first year of the move, the government thought it would be a good idea for me to retire with a small pension, allowing a younger person to have my job. I went back to Quảng Ngãi with Thuy.

At this point, Mai looked sad and spoke slowly. She didn't go into much detail about why she was replaced.

Maybe I'll skip over some of the next years. I worked a series of small jobs, but I want to get to one of the interesting times in my saga.

When Thuy was about six years old, Tuan came to visit me to ask for my permission to marry a woman from his hometown. Tuan's fiancée had a small shop in Duc Pho. Of course, Tuan hadn't told her that he had a child with me.

I discussed the dilemma with my Communist cell members. It was a complicated issue. I could bear more children, but I also recognized my limitations in being able to care for more than one child. Tuan was the eldest son of his large family clan. His father had two wives, and Tuan had eight siblings. The family dragon fruit farm was doing well, and it was time for Tuan to take over its management from his father. I had a lot of leverage over Tuan. If he married without my permission, I could damage his reputation. But the just and right decision, I felt, was to release him voluntarily from the bond with me. And that was my decision, to let him go so he could fulfill his filial duties and live a full life. We parted on friendly terms.

Tuan stayed in touch with me and always sent money for Thuy. From time to time, there would be an excuse for the three of us to see one another. Then in the summer of 1986,

Tuan was assigned to attend a teacher training program in Quảng Ngãi, and he came to live with Thuy and me. It was a happy time for all of us.

Tuan's Wife Discovers He Is Living with Mai

When Tuan's wife heard the rumor that he was living with me, she literally jumped up and caught a bus to Quảng Ngãi. It's more than a five-hour trip by bus, so she didn't arrive until nearly 6 p.m. Tuan was in the kitchen helping me cook, and Thuy was playing around us. The wife, then three months pregnant, was a furious dragon. She raged and made a riot of noise. She yelled and kicked a pan on the floor. She grabbed a broom and hit it on the table. Everyone in the neighborhood—since the walls of our houses touched each other—heard her words of anger. Thuy clung to her father's pant leg, saying, "Papa, Papa, what's wrong?" Tuan left us and followed his wife out of the house. They went by bike to his wife's relative's house. They talked for a few hours and then came back to my house so his wife could confirm that Tuan was being truthful.

Jane, you know me. I can be a logical and persuasive talker. I explained to Tuan's wife the whole history of our relationship and why Thuy was born. I also made it clear that I had released Tuan from any obligations when he told me he wanted to marry her. I advised her, "Forgive Tuan. Forget his history. He was wrong not to tell you, but he is your husband now. Accept that and be happy."

Later that night, Tuan's wife went to stay with her relatives. As a parting gesture, when Tuan's wife left for Qui Nhon the next day, I assured her that my nieces, the two student nurses boarding with me, would act as chaperones to assure that nothing happened between Tuan and me. Tuan did, however, continue to stay with me and Thuy until his training program finished.

Tuan's wife gave birth to the baby she was carrying when she stormed into my house. They named him Huong. When Huong was about five years old, Tuan's wife came with Huong and spent one and a half months in Tam Ky with me. She had longed for a little girl to spoil, so she brought many gifts for Thuy to enjoy. She loved combing Thuy's hair and attaching barrettes. Tuan and his wife eventually had their own daughter. Years later, when Thuy was studying in Saigon, she stayed with her half sister who had a good job with a foreign country. Even now, Thuy and her half brother Huong are particularly close.

Just to attest what a fine man Tuan is, I want to tell you about the time when Thuy and Long got married. Long traveled to Qui Nhon to ask Tuan for permission to marry his daughter. Then Tuan traveled to Quảng Ngãi to represent his daughter to the patriarch of Long's family. Tuan praised his daughter's beauty and intelligence. By then, Thuy was working at the television station, and Tuan told Long's parents that they should be patient with Thuy because she was a working professional outside of the home. This was a new phenomenon in Vietnam, as you know. Tuan explained, "I hope you will appreciate that Thuy won't be able to accomplish as much traditional hard housework that many parents-in-laws expect of their daughters-in-law because she has another job." What do you think, Jane? Tuan is a pretty enlightened man, no?

I was proud to be with Tuan at the wedding. We made a fine couple, though he was forty-eight and I was fifty-eight. When I show you the wedding pictures, you will see a handsome man wearing a traditional silk ao dai reaching his knees, with matching pants and a wrapped headdress of black silk. I wore a velvet jacket. Thuy was, of course, in a red ao dai—the color of good fortune and happiness—and was even wearing lipstick for the occasion. We were a happy family on an auspicious day.

Tuan gave Thuy three gold rings. Thuy has traveled several times over the years to visit Tuan and his family. Tuan's parents are fond of Thuy, and the grandmother, as recently as last summer, reminded Thuy that she must return to the grandmother's village to be with her when her husband dies. I can proudly state that there has never been any prejudice or negative attitudes toward Thuy because her mother and father were not married.

While we were in Hanoi, Mai was contacted by two journalists. One was from the large newspaper, *Youth*. Its circulation was 500,000 copies a day, and we knew it was one of the most popular papers in Vietnam. The other journalist was from the celebrated *World Peace*. They came to the house, on separate occasions, and it was such fun for us to weave together the story of how we met and why we were close friends. I saw the articles and photographs six months later when Mai mailed them.

Article about Mai, Jane and Sophie in Vietnamese newspaper

Letter from Mai After the Hanoi Visit

Sophie and I were sad to leave Mai, but we needed to return to our other lives—mine in historic preservation and fundraising and Sophie's as a Vietnamese history professor at Temple University. Mai returned to her post office position in Tam Ky with many happy memories of Hanoi. A month later I received this letter:

> *Dear Jane, my little sister, my most precious friend of all!*
>
> *July 7, 2005, was the day we parted, a very sad Hanoi autumn day. I got on the plane, but I couldn't bring myself to look back at you one last time. Beloved Jane! I do know that you are very busy. Lots of work has come your way. You work all the time and with great skill. Sophie told me this. Wouldn't it be nice if I could be there to assist you in some small way? The two newspapers, Youth and World Peace, have been printed. I've read them. They are quite well written, though a bit sloppy in a couple of places, but that doesn't matter. All my friends like to read these papers, and they have written letters and called to wish me joy and exclaim over my meaningful and moving trip. We had such a wonderful feeling of togetherness, the three of us, and I am grateful for the warmth you and Sophie feel toward me. Everybody feels that the sympathy you two feel for me is rarely found. It is unique and unequaled in this world.*
>
> *Lots of people who didn't know me well ask, "Why do these American women love you so much? How do they know you? How is it that they can speak Vietnamese? How did they know you were in Tam Ky? These two American women are smart, eh? Did they eat meals with you? Did they stay at your place? Were they able to take it on our hard beds? Boy, did they put up with a lot, eh? Where did they take a shower? Did they use chopsticks?"*
>
> *My close friends asked about me. The news stories made them choke up, and people said, "Reading that story made me*

come out in goose bumps all over, Mai is to be pitied, and even though they are Americans, they can love a Vietnamese so deeply, hmm?" Lots of phone calls from friends in Hanoi, Saigon, and Danang, asking about my trip, which was most unusual.

Beloved Jane! I sit here doing my little job with the phone company. I'm really missing you. You and Sophie are models for my daughter Thuy—you are women of deep feeling, meaningfulness, and competence.

To end my letter, I wish for you a life that is happy, full of meaning for this world, for a world at peace.

Love to you, Chi Mai

CHAPTER 16

Tracing the Diarist's Footsteps

Decades after journalist Frances FitzGerald made her foray into the liberated territories of Quảng Ngãi, our paths crossed again. She had been asked to write an introduction to *Last Night I Dreamed of Peace: The Diary of Dang Thuy Tram*, written during the war by a female North Vietnamese doctor. Frances and Harmony Books, an imprint of Random House Publishers, hired me just as Harmony was beginning the process of publishing the journal in English and, eventually, at least sixteen other languages. My role was to travel to Vietnam, gather background information about Thuy Tram, and visit Duc Pho, where she was killed by American soldiers. I spent hours talking about the diary with Fred Whitehurst, a former US intelligence officer, and his brother Rob, who facilitated returning a copy of it to the young doctor's family. They filled me in on details of their trip to meet the Trams and travel to Duc Pho. I told Mai I was coming.

Dang Thuy Tram

Thirty-five years earlier, Fred was assigned to an American military unit that discovered an abandoned, underground hospital in the jungle. He had the authority to decide which captured documents to preserve or burn. Among them was a handmade diary with cardboard covers cut from a box of medicines and pages sewn together with string. It was small enough to fit in a pocket. Fred's interpreter picked up the diary, thumbed through it, and said, "Don't burn this, Fred. There is fire in it already."[47]

Over a few sweltering nights, in a tent back at the firebase, the interpreter read the diary to Fred. He learned Thuy Tram had volunteered to serve as a physician with the NLF in the south and help the revolutionary efforts against the Americans and South Vietnamese military forces. She followed her sweetheart, who had also gone from North to South Vietnam. The "fire" in her daily accounts included poetry detailing frightening and emotional episodes of life in a war zone. "Human to human, I fell in love with her," he later said.[48]

Fred took the diary back to the US and, decades later, miraculously returned a copy to Thuy's mother, who hadn't known the fate of her daughter. Through email correspondence, she told Fred how grateful she was for "bringing my daughter's voice back to me" and asked if she could consider Fred "her son." Fred began to call her "Mother Tram." She told Fred, "You and my daughter were both patriots, just on opposite sides of the war."[49]

Fred donated the original diary to Texas Tech University in Lubbock and invited Mother Tram and Thuy's three sisters to the US to hold the journal in their hands. They first traveled to North Carolina to meet Fred's mother, about the same age as Mother Tram, before continuing to Texas. When the Trams insisted on paying their own way, Fred reminded her, "If you are really my mother, then you must—at least—let your son pay for your ticket."

Fred believed the diary embodied the soul of a brave young woman whose saga could humanize the war for Vietnamese and Americans. He encouraged Mother Tram and her daughters to have it published. Fred was from a military family, had served three tours in Vietnam, and Rob had also served in Vietnam. If Fred could cross the line to love his enemy, he thought other readers might have similar sympathies.

---

47 Dang Thuy Tram, *Last Night I Dreamed of Peace: The Diary of Dang Thuy Tram*, Harmony Books, September 2007, Introduction, Francis FitzGerald, p. XVI.
48 Ibid, p. XVI
49 Whitehurst, Robert, *Finding Thuy*, manuscript, p. 98.

Mother Tram and her daughters insisted Thuy was only doing her part in the war effort, like thousands of other youth who volunteered, and Thuy should not be glorified above anyone else. When they eventually conceded to publishing the diary in Vietnam, it sold over 430,000 copies, more than any other publication in the country's history. By that time, over 75 percent of Vietnam's population had been born after the war, and their knowledge of the conflict came from textbooks or elders who had lived through the violence. Young readers were captivated hearing the story through the voice of someone their age, a peer, a woman who wrote in a brutally honest style. Thuy exposed her strengths, vulnerabilities, and changing emotions as she experienced war.

> **26 November 1968:** *It is my birthday and the sound of the enemy's guns reverberates in all directions. I am used to helping wounded soldiers evade the enemy, wearing a heavy backpack on my shoulders. It is nothing. Two arduous years have hardened me to the bullets and the fire of war.*[50]

In 2005 when the Whitehurst brothers went to Vietnam to meet the Trams, they were greeted at the airport by a crowd of journalists and people bearing flowers. They met the prime minister and were interviewed on television. The nation embraced Thuy's story.

Before any trip to Vietnam, critical prep work includes the purchase of appropriate gifts. Gift-giving is an important aspect of Vietnamese culture, and Rob, particularly, helped me identify gifts for the family, although I couldn't match his cleverness. He bought socks with amusing motifs, and indeed, in the colder months, when the sisters and Mother Tram wore them with sandals, Rob got a kick out of seeing photos with little ducks or red chili peppers peeking from beneath their trouser legs.

I knew from the diary that Thuy's father was a surgeon. Her mother was a professor of pharmacology with a specialty in herbal medicine.

---

50 Dang Thuy Tram, *Last Night I Dreamed of Peace: The Diary of Dang Thuy Tram*, Harmony Books, September 2007, p. 69.

Thuy had attended an elite high school, founded in 1906 by the French, who built colonial-style buildings surrounded by a walled courtyard and gracious trees. She and her sisters were highly educated.

The family lived in Hanoi, in a narrow, four-story house down a series of alleyways. Kim, the diarist's youngest sister and an engineer by training, knew the house would be impossible to find. She waited at a main street intersection and guided me through the maze. Mother Tram, a dignified, white-haired woman, said going up and down the stairs of the family home kept her agile. She grew up during French occupation, when the language of the educated was French, and she enjoyed speaking French with me. Kim emailed in advance,

> Maybe I need to tell you something about my family so you can imagine how Thuy lived before going south. Before the revolution [1945], my family was prosperous. We had maids, servants, and lived the way of a bourgeois family. When ... the war against the French broke out, my parents left ... and went to the countryside. ... We lived like everybody in the country, except that we kept all interest in trivial things like books, flowers, music, art. ... We received limited rations, 0.3 kg of rice per month. But at times we agreed to exchange that ration for a music disk or book. My mother always tells us to keep the spirit rich. The salary of a doctor and professor was not different from a worker at that time. ... Sometimes we had not enough food. The whole family of seven people lived in one room, in a thatch cottage. But in that room, we still got [sic] flowers, music, paintings. ... And now, as you can see, we can say that our life is so-so.[51]

Indeed, when I sat in the living room with Mother Tram, there were multiple book-filled shelves behind her. Framed photographs

---

51 Whitehurst, Robert, *Finding Thuy*, manuscript, email from Kim Tran to Fred Whitehurst, p. 4.

were placed on tables, and paintings hung on the wall. A cat snuggled in her lap. The sisters came to the house to meet me, and we went to a restaurant where their spouses and children filled chairs at a long table. I struggled to match names and faces. The next days were spent talking about Thuy Tram, learning more about the family, and locating sights, including Thuy's private high school.

I felt connected to Thuy, and there were parallels in our stories. We had worked in South Vietnam during the same years. Her underground hospital and the site where she was shot were just a few miles from the AFSC Rehabilitation Center. Not only were we nearly the same age, living in adjoining districts, but we were both volunteers with civilian projects. She began working in public health and initially trained local citizens in the south to improve community health and promote best practices in obstetrics. As the war intensified, Thuy served as a doctor to guerrilla soldiers and North Vietnamese sailors,[52] while I directed a medical-Rehabilitation Center. I was retracing the steps of a sister.

Thuy's sisters, Kim and Phuong, embarked on the train from Hanoi to Danang with me. I stayed in a small hotel, and the sisters stayed with a friend. Since Thuy was a celebrity—her diary, a bestseller, and the story were covered extensively in the national media—there was a buzz when the concierge excitedly told the other staff that I knew the Trams. When Kim came to pick me up, they clustered in corners of the lobby to peek at the sister of the famous diarist.

We picked up Mai in a hired van and continued south to the small town of Duc Pho. I had been there frequently. The war had been fierce, and many of our patients came from the area. But this was a new experience, to travel with such accomplished women. The Tram family was worldly, with deep cultural and educational traditions,

---

52 North Vietnam established the HCM Sea Trail to successfully transport thousands of supplies, medicine, and military equipment to the South. The boats were called Nameless Ships because they often had no registration numbers. Thuy Tram's mother was, coincidentally, watching a documentary on her seventieth birthday about these ships. A picture of Thuy Tram appeared on the screen, and a sea captain was recorded complimenting how Thuy and her clinic had saved his injured sailors when the ship was sunk by the enemy.

different from the more rural, less educated population I knew in Quảng Ngãi. The Quảng Ngãi people might not have had formal academic education, but many, like Mai, were wise.

Breakfast on the rooftop terrace was genteel, and Mai mixed well with the company. It was one thing for Mai to mingle with and befriend the Western staff who worked at the AFSC Rehab Center but, I imagine, quite a different experience socializing with educated, sophisticated Vietnamese. It might have been her first encounter with people from Hanoi, and I wondered if Phuong and Kim felt enriched by meeting Mai, typical of the revolutionary country people who were comrades of their sister.

There were some tricky moments. The hotel stairs were slippery and too numerous for Mai to navigate. She had never been in an elevator and was frightened of the "moving box," distrustful of what supported it in the air. She learned to like it, exclaiming, "Elevators make the stairs so easy for me."

The sisters and I met with government officials to outline our visit and intentions. The Duc Pho district in Quảng Ngãi Province had a long history of resistance to foreign occupiers, and the French never gained control of the city or most of the province. During my time, the US and South Vietnamese usually had authority over the main highway, although it often closed because of fighting. However, they did not control the flatlands on the ocean side of the highway or the mountains on the other side.

In her diary, Thuy described walking at night to being in a play.

> *On a night emergency aid mission . . . lights from the [American] bases shine brightly from three directions around me, and flares hang in midair in front of me. The light sources cast my shadows in different directions, and I feel like an actor on stage, as in the days when I was still a medical student performing in a play. Now I am also an actor on the stage of life.*[53]

---

53 Dang Thuy Tram, *Last Night I Dreamed of Peace: The Diary of Dang Thuy Tram*, New York, Harmony Books, 2017, p. 146.

During the visit to Duc Pho with Mai and Thuy's sisters, I met the patient Thuy refers to on the first page of her diary, Huynh Doan Sang, who was sixty-seven years old. He lifted his shirt to show me the scar where Thuy had operated, but then he rushed home to tend his noodle stand, as it was nearing noon, his busiest hour of the day.

> **8 April 1968:** *Operated on one case . . . with inadequate anesthesia. I had only a few meager vials of Novocain to give the soldier, but he never groaned once during the entire procedure. He even smiled to encourage me. Seeing that forced smile on lips withered by exhaustion, I empathized with him immensely. . . . Brushing the stray hair back from his forehead, I wanted to say, "If I cannot even heal people like you, this sorrow will not fade from my medical career."*[54]

That evening Mai and I talked late into the night about Thuy's and our experiences. Thuy vividly described the brutality of war.

> *This morning, they bring me a wounded soldier, [Khanh]; a phosphorous bomb has burned his entire body. An hour after he is hit, skin is still burning, smoke rising from his body. Nobody recognizes him as the cheerful, handsome young man he once was. Today his smiling joyful black eyes have been reduced to two little holes—the yellow eyelids are cooked. The reeking burn of phosphorus smoke still rises from his body. He looks as if he has been roasted in an oven. I stand frozen before this heartbreaking tableau. His mother weeps. Her trembling hands touch her son's body: pieces of skin fall off, curled up like crumbling sheets of rice cracker.*[55]

---

54 Ibid, p. 4.
55 Ibid, p. 142.

My experience was witnessing children brought to the Rehab Center with napalm burns. One was an eight-year-old girl whose burn was so deep, her shin bone was exposed. Burn patients at the Center soaked their wounds in a large bath and were given physical therapy exercises to keep the muscles and flesh flexible.

From time to time, I visited the burn ward. I'm not afraid of mice or snakes, but the first time I saw maggots squirming on the wounds of patients, I was horrified. Though maggots appeared because of inadequate nursing care, lack of bandages, and unclean conditions, Mai and I learned years later that they are extremely efficient at removing dead tissue in wounds. What disgusted us at the time was, in fact, therapeutic.

Mai was exposed to Agent Orange, the herbicide that killed vegetation and poisoned the land. Thuy's diary details its effects.

> *The forest is gouged and scarred by bombs; the remaining trees stained yellow by toxic chemicals. We're affected by the poison, too. All cadres are severely fatigued, their arms and legs weary, their appetites gone. They can neither move nor eat. We want to encourage one another but there are moments when . . . the shadow of pessimism creeps upon us.*[56]

Mai knew many American soldiers were affected by Agent Orange but hadn't realized those who handled the toxic chemical were still fighting the government to acknowledge it had been the cause of their cancers. Since Vietnamese people and land were the intended victims of napalm, Mai expressed her sadness: "Agent Orange was an invisible weapon that has killed Vietnamese and Americans."

Both Mai and Thuy spent time in tunnels dug by the Vietnamese during the war. Some were small, for a single person. Others were cleverly designed and layered mini-towns, large enough to hold water buffalo or schoolrooms for children. As a doctor, Thuy occasionally

---

56 Ibid, p. 125.

received special treatment with access to a particularly secret chamber. She wrote about someone bailing water from her underground tunnel in case she had to jump into it. Mai laughed, recalling again when she and another cadre hid in a tunnel filled with red ants.

Mai described a tunnel she often used.

> I would dive into the river holding my breath, feeling for underground posts that marked the opening to the tunnel. I squeezed my body up through the muddy, water-filled tunnel to reach the area inside the riverbank where I would be above water. I always thought my lungs would burst before I reached the air pocket. Once, I couldn't hold my breath. My mouth and lungs were full of muddy water, and I lay on the tunnel floor, gasping for air, before I recovered. Then I would crawl on my stomach along a long tunnel that led to a larger "room" carved out of the earth. The transition from the tunnel to the room was tricky as I arrived in the space headfirst. I'd tumble down the slope to the floor of the hideaway. In this space, there was even a small stove to dry my clothes. Long bamboo pipes carried the smoke in several directions to disperse it into wisps of smoke too small to call the attention of the Americans.

The Dang Thuy Tram Clinic is an impressive structure for the small town of Duc Pho. It includes a museum and, outside, a statue of Thuy in Vietnamese style pants and a shirt, with a *non* (conical hat) tilted back on her head. The sculpture, in the Soviet realism style, shows her as a colossal woman in midstride, not exactly like the photos I saw at the Tram home. The clinic works with disabled children born to parents exposed to Agent Orange. Besides causing cancer, it altered the genes of those heavily exposed, causing deformities in their children. Because Thuy had written about the horrors of Agent Orange, her family wanted these patients prioritized.

The clinic was two years old, clean and modern. The director recounted the story of Dr. Tram and the goals of the clinic. One of my tasks was to gather photos and permissions for the English version of Thuy's diary. I took special notice of exhibit photographs to find any not already in the family collection, but the family had already provided me with everything I needed.

When Rob Whitehurst attended the clinic's dedication ceremony, he planted daylilies, of different colors and styles, from his mother's garden. Rob asked me to check on them. Knowing Mother Tram's passion for flowers, I was touched by the daylilies—a gesture from a soldier's mother to a patriot's mother—representing reconciliation and peace between the Whitehurst brothers and the Tram family. Thuy wrote about her love of flowers—and peace:

> *I see it now . . . the flowers of victory and heroism are blooms of flesh and bones of many young lives. I am walking . . . in the middle of that flower garden, my heart filling with so much admiration, pride and immense pain when each flower falls. I have always loved flowers, but now with each step, my appreciation for the true beauty of FLOWERS has given me a deeper understanding of love, hate and pride.*[57]

The woman who wrote these words and cared for civilians and soldiers in this region became a folk hero. Young people and government officials were in awe of her. I was fortunate to be in the company of the Trams as they toured the clinic and were hosted by government officials and clinic workers at a celebratory dinner. I've had many wonderful meals in my life (and written two cookbooks), but no food was as delicious as the delicate, local freshwater fish served that day. Perhaps my heightened emotions made the food so delectable. I was walking in Thuy's footsteps.

The next morning, Kim, Phuong, and I were driven to the base of

---

57   Ibid, p. 64.

a mountain trail. It was serene and cool. Kim found some white lilies, Thuy's favorite, to bring along. We walked on level ground and took a boat across a river. We were in the region of the H're, one of many minority tribes in Vietnam. It was a H're man who found and buried Thuy's body along the jungle path. Once across the river, the route led into the mountains.

When I lived in Quảng Ngãi, I often looked toward the deep blue-black mountains. They were close but unreachable since they were under the control of the NLF. Finally, it was my turn to enjoy them in the province where I had worked for nearly three years. The trek was breathtaking. It was still early in the morning but already hot. Rob and Fred said they were barely strong enough to make this trip, but we three trotted along at a good pace. Phuong and Kim stopped along the way to point out plants and herbs. Mother Tram, with her vast knowledge, had taught her daughters about medicinal plants. Kim and Phuong had made this walk before to exhume Thuy's body and place it in a coffin to take to Hanoi. Only then did Kim realize Thuy had been shot through the forehead.

Fred said the American Division had placed Thuy on a targeted execution list. It seems the presence of a female North Vietnamese doctor in the jungle, treating the enemy, was demoralizing to US troops. Kim said knowing that Thuy, a doctor dedicated to saving human lives, had been brutally killed was the hardest part to accept.

When we reached the place where Thuy died, we placed the lilies on the path and then sat and meditated. We lit incense and invoked her memory. As Thuy's diary ends, the enemy had destroyed her clinic, and she was waiting for reinforcements and help. Her comrades evacuated most of the wounded on stretchers. Thuy and two female nurses remained behind to tend those who were too wounded to be moved.

> **June 20, 1970:** *Still, no one comes. It has been almost ten days since the second bombardment.... The enemy is certainly nearby. [I am] here with five non-ambulatory wounded*

> soldiers. If the enemy comes, there is nothing we can do but run. Nien, the injured young soldier, tells us, "Sincerely, be calm, Sisters. Run if the enemy comes. We will stay and fight them to the death."[58]

I know Kim and Phuong agonized over Thuy's last words.

> I am no longer a child. I have grown up. I have passed trials of peril, but somehow at this moment, I yearn deeply for Mother's caring hand. Come to me, squeeze my hand, know my loneliness, and give me the love, the strength to prevail on the perilous road before me.[59]

An American military report later confirmed Thuy's comrades had sent reinforcements and the wounded soldiers were evacuated, but Thuy was already dead. Being at the exact place where she died, mourning her, I wondered what was going through her sisters' minds. When we were ready, we continued to the top of the mountain to a small memorial for Thuy, where many readers of the diary had come to pay homage by leaving notes and mementos.

As we retraced our path, taking the same boat across the river, we saw H're people tending water buffalo. Once, this place was the scene of fighting and death, but now water lapped the sides of the boat and the animals moved slowly in the mud.

Return to Tam Ky & Hanoi

On the ride back to Tam Ky, I asked Mai if she would consider coming to the US. Our government had been the aggressor, and American mines had caused her to lose her legs, but Mai was always careful to say, "I am not at war with the American people, just the American government," the same words I heard years ago in an

---

58   Ibid, p. 222.
59   Ibid, p. 225.

NLF village from the mysterious Uncle Nam. Mai responded with a question of her own: "Would I be in danger of being arrested because I am a Communist Party member?"

I assured her the war was over. She was considering my question. How would she get the money for a plane ticket? Would she be frightened to take such a long trip? Where would she go in the US? There were many questions to answer together.

When we got to Tam Ky, the driver asked for Mai's address and drove to the house. At first, Mai didn't recognize it, which startled me. Then I realized she always approached it on the back of a scooter. Being up high in the van gave her a different vantage point. I hoped this trip, tracing the life of a fellow freedom fighter, would expand other horizons for her. Mai and I embraced. We weren't sure when we would meet again.

As Kim, Phuong, and I traveled to Hanoi, the sound of the train wheels made my thoughts ricochet. In the following days, I visited Martyrs Cemetery, where Thuy Tram's body was buried, and the Tram country house. I was adopted by a Vietnamese family.

CHAPTER 17

Agent Orange

Returning to the US, I coordinated various aspects of the publication of the English version of *Last Night I Dreamed of Peace: The Diary of Dang Thuy Tram*, including obtaining permission for photographic reproduction from the original sources. I also wrote over 300 footnotes. I was living through Thuy's words. I scrutinized every page for places or people that might require a footnote. A year and a half later, the diary was in print.

It was an international success, translated into sixteen languages and often compared to the diary of Anne Frank. Francine Prose reviewed the book in *O, The Oprah Magazine*, saying it "offers a rare combination of lyricism, grit, passion and humanity." While an average printing in Vietnam was about 2,000 copies, sales rose to nearly half a million. Young Vietnamese devoured the book. Inside was a twenty-seven-year-old woman, someone close to their age, telling them about the war, even criticizing the Communist Party for not accepting her as a member. They identified with her.

There were two sets of readers regardless of nationality: those who knew little about the Vietnam War and those deeply familiar, who had followed newspaper and television reports. Sam, a friend and US Army veteran, emailed me about his personal trauma from wartime experiences, saying it caused him to live in silence for decades. He was frozen in the present and hadn't been able to visit his past until he read Thuy's words. Although his experience as an officer was different from Thuy's as a doctor for the NLF, she represented universal values he admired. Sam wrote he "felt a sense of reconciliation in reading the book. It allowed me to forgive myself."

I wanted to honor Thuy and established a nonprofit to raise funds for the Dang Thuy Tram Clinic, specifically for Agent Orange victims. Frances FitzGerald served on the board and wrote one of the first checks. A former antiwar activist attorney donated his services to guide me through the legal process. As people read the book, some found the Thuy Tram Fund online and sent money.

I emailed Kim Tram to ask her what I should do with the funds. Moving them to the clinic seemed logical. However, the Vietnamese government covered the operational cost for government facilities and hospitals, and I wasn't sure if a private donation would be accepted. Kim assured me the gift would be welcome. I could deliver the funds to Vietnam, and Kim would transfer them to the operating budget of the clinic.

I contacted Mai about the fundraising effort. She knew people on the Agent Orange Committee for Quang Nam (the province next to Quảng Ngãi). I wasn't sure what she had in mind. She said a teaching colleague from her early days with the NLF was on the committee and would have ideas. So, as often happens when it comes to Vietnam, I didn't have the full story of what was in store for me when I traveled to Hanoi a few months later. I trusted my Vietnamese friends to guide me.

Although it had only been three years since I was last in Vietnam, tourism was making a huge impact. Tour buses squeezed through Hanoi's Old Quarter—on streets established a thousand years ago—to accommodate foot traffic. The city seemed more polluted than I remembered, but the old joys were still there—eating at sidewalk stalls, admiring flowers sold on the street by bicycle vendors, and enjoying casual conversations with Vietnamese people I met.

My first stop was to visit the Tram family. It was sentimental and productive. The sentimental part was visiting with Mother Tram. She was in good health and spirits and exuded serenity and humor, almost like a Buddhist monk. I brought amaryllis bulbs for her from the US (although I suspect it was not legal to transfer agricultural products). Mother Tram kept a large rooftop garden of plants with multiple textures and colors and healing herbs unknown to me. I was glad to add my flowers to her collection. The productive part was finalizing the fund transfer to the clinic.

A few days later, I traveled to meet Mai. She had traveled with me and the Tram sisters to the site of Thuy Tram's death and had read *Last Night I Dreamed of Peace* in Vietnamese. She fully understood my mission. Mai had come to appreciate American philanthropy by working for AFSC, which accepted no US government funds and operated on the generous donations of individuals, and knew why I was arriving in Vietnam with "private" money.

Mai understood that the bulk of the money was going to the clinic, but I asked if small gifts could be given to victims of Agent Orange in her local area. She quickly got down to business. The Quang Nam Agent Orange Committee determined—unknown to me—that certain, deserving individuals would receive small loans, not gifts. Mai's NLF teacher-colleague, Mr. Nam, arrived with another member of the committee, with information about families who could benefit from a microloan. Repayment of the loan would generate a return that could help someone else.

The committee wanted to take me to visit Agent Orange victims and asked me to present an envelope of money to each recipient. I was pleased with the committee's work but did not want to be the "great White benefactor" doling out money. I felt the committee should give out the funds since they had selected the recipients.

Mai went into her persuasive mode.

> Jane, everyone in Vietnam knows these poisonous chemicals came from the US. You aren't part of the government that sprayed our people and land. But the people of Quảng Ngãi will appreciate that some Americans are taking

responsibility for Agent Orange if you—an American—hand them an envelope of money. They will understand and be glad that an American is involved in atoning for the damage. You are not paying for restitution; you are making a gesture of reconciliation for the future of our two countries.

Mai had made up her mind, and it was only a matter of time until I saw her point of view. I wasn't comfortable playing this role to people severely deformed by Agent Orange, but if, in their eyes, I was offering reconciliation, then I was prepared to take it on.

To my amazement, Mai and the committee had already determined specific sums for each family. Inside each envelope, the recipient found a document to sign confirming a certain percentage rate and payback date—or series of dates—and eventually, the whole sum would allow other Agent Orange victims to benefit.

Mai, once again, had pulled off one of her plans. I thought of some of the fiascos of other nonprofit agencies: delivering goods that weren't appropriate, hiring staff who abused people they were intended to help, and preventing money from reaching the victims in need. Mai was smart and efficient. She and her colleagues had done their research.

I asked how they could be sure victims were suffering from Agent Orange and not another disease, a question coming a bit late in the process. Yet, the committee members carefully answered my question, explaining they had matched the location of the victim during the war with research marking areas where Agent Orange had defoliated the landscape.

Still not liking the idea that I would be the center of attention as I handed out the envelopes, I gritted my teeth and got on the back of an old Vespa belonging to a committee member. Mr. Nam told me not to ride sidesaddle, the way Mai rode since her prosthetic legs gave her no other choice. He encouraged me to straddle the seat, explaining we would be going over rough areas.

We launched into the maze of humanity on Route 1—where

trucks, cars, and people were walking, riding bikes, and carrying large loads balanced on poles. Animals and children mingled with the action swarming around us. *Did that truck really pass us on the right with tires almost in the rice paddy?* Occasionally, vehicles drove on the wrong side of the road if less traffic was coming toward them. The ride was terrifying, but soon we were on dirt roads and paths. I understood what Mr. Nam meant. Rain had created potholes with muddy, slippery edges we either had to drive through or navigate around. I only fell off once.

Memories of the people damaged by Agent Orange have stayed with me. I have come to terms with the fact that my government tortured prisoners. "Torture" was at least war terminology I was familiar with. The policy of using chemicals to destroy and deform humans, including US soldiers, was an exceptionally cruel part of the Vietnam War. It is estimated that nearly twelve million gallons of Agent Orange were dropped on free-fire zones.

We first visited a teenager whose mother had been in a free-fire zone. He had a skin condition so raw and painful, he preferred not to have fabric touching his skin even in cold weather. He was a genius with machines and had set up a makeshift motor bike repair operation under a tarp. His loan would go toward building a simple structure to protect him from monsoon rains and oppressive heat while he worked. He was a lively, young man with a supportive family.

The next loan went to a couple whose eight-year-old had severe deformities. The child had one eye, contorted facial features, and thin limbs that protruded at angles. She was a bit wild and, in the past, managed to climb out windows. Once, she was almost killed by traffic. The parents needed to take turns caring for their daughter while running their small restaurant, and the loan would be used to build a room where she could play without hurting herself. At first, I wondered if this solution was designed to hide or lock away a maimed child, but I observed two loving parents who doted on their daughter. Mai assured me that she and Mr. Nam, or another member of the committee, would visit all loan recipients to confirm that the conditions of support were being fulfilled.

We visited six other families, and I was always offered the first cup of tea. They were dignified and polite, and no one asked for pity. Mai and Mr. Nam had visited them before and helped me feel at ease. Later, three of us visited another senior member of the Quang Nam Agent Orange Committee to report on the day's activities.

The next morning, Mai's daughter, Thuy, and her husband, Long, took me to a coffee shop. Previously, these didn't exist in Tam Ky. The shop was decorated with plants and equipped with normal-sized tables and chairs, rather than little stools. Vietnamese coffee is delicious, and I welcomed this contemporary addition to the city.

I told Mai that working jointly on a project—giving loans to Agent Orange victims—was like old times at the AFSC Rehabilitation Center. Only this time, the project was our own initiative. Mai was profoundly committed to her country. She had willingly joined the revolution and had become disabled as a result. I, too, was passionate about Vietnam. I rejoiced that nearly forty years after we met, we were joined in a mutual project to help its people.

Friends and family dropped in later, including Thuy, her husband, and Mai's grandchildren. I, with only one sibling and no grandchildren or nieces and nephews, particularly appreciated being with them; my family gatherings were always small. At this lovely get together in Vietnam, we did nothing—which meant we did everything that was important in life: sharing love, talking, and eating. We made our usual promises to meet again before we died, though reality weighed heavily on us.

I headed back to Hanoi to report on my trip to Mother Tram and Kim. Traveling alone suited me. But I was shaken. Although I'd seen a lot of death and destruction during the war, firsthand exposure to the grim aftermath of bodies twisted and deformed by Agent Orange shocked me. The US government has made few attempts at reparation for the damage to the people or land.

CHAPTER 18

Bonded

Mai Comes to the US

Over the next few years, Mai and I kept in touch via email. No more lost letters. Mai accepted my offer to come to the US, and arrangements snowballed into a major logistical operation. The biggest hurdle was securing a visa for Mai's daughter, Thuy. The embassy refused to issue a visa to a young Vietnamese woman who might seek to remain in the US. After a few former AFSC Vietnam staff wrote letters to the embassy explaining the purpose of the trip, Thuy and Mai received visas.

Mai allowed us to buy only one ticket. A couple of us, who had come to know Mai well through the AFSC Rehab Center project, had planned to share the cost of both. After some discussion, we agreed to Mai's conditions.

> I am always aware of the fact that the US economic situation is better than ours in Vietnam. But please keep in mind that I try not to depend on friends, because if I did, the friendship would not last long. I want our friendship to last forever, forever beautiful, into the lives of our offspring.

Our position of privilege may allow us to be generous, but sometimes that can separate us. Friendship levels the field. Mai had never asked for favors or money. She was our equal.

Was this plan to have Mai—and Thuy—come to the US a bit

crazy? Thuy said she got carsick. Mai might hate American food. And how would Mai react to a country that had killed family members and friends, delayed Vietnamese independence for years, and was responsible for the land mine that took her legs?

I was concerned how Mai would contend with the nearly sixteen-hour flight, including getting from her seat to the bathroom. Thuy contacted the airline for assistance, and the flight from Ho Chi Minh City to San Francisco went smoothly. We located a used wheelchair in good condition, and it was waiting for Mai in California. (Her old wheelchair was beaten up, and we hoped she would take this newer one back to Vietnam, which she did.)

Mai and Thuy were greeted by former AFSC staff Claudia Krich and Keith Brinton, directors who succeeded David and me in Quảng Ngãi. They drove Mai and Thuy to their home in Davis, California. Mai and Thuy loved the warm weather and lush vegetation. Keith and Claudia had family nearby, including Claudia's ninety-year-old parents. Mai said it felt like an extended Vietnamese family.

From there, Mai and Thuy flew to Washington, DC, where I was living. Mai was particularly curious about the nation's capital, which she saw as the military and political center for the war. One of the first things they, my daughter Maria Mai, and I did was visit the Vietnam Veterans Memorial Wall. I sometimes pushed Mai in her US wheelchair on long stretches, but when we arrived at the wall, she wanted to navigate by herself.

The V-shaped wall is often described as a slash deep into the earth since it is sited below ground. As Mai rolled down the sidewalk parallel to the wall, she looked, panel by panel, at the rows and rows of names. At first, she was silent. Finally, she said,

> The enormity of loss is evident in all those American names. Americans should have understood the Vietnamese would never have stopped fighting for our independence. None of these young men and women needed to have died. As for us, so many

were lost, we couldn't even gather all their names for a wall. Men, women, children. Many of my friends' bodies were never recovered. None of this had to happen.

I considered what Mai said. In America, we are oriented to the individual, and listing the name of each lost life reflected that. For Mai, Vietnam had lost so many people, it wasn't possible to list them all; they shared a collective bond. It was "we," not "I."

This was why working in the Rehabilitation Center was not a depressing experience. No matter one's political sympathies, the patients felt part of a whole—the whole country was suffering—and they were grateful to walk again and help their families and villages in some capacity. After the war, Vietnam looked forward. It was different for American soldiers. They went to war as individuals. Sometimes they formed deep connections with buddies, and sometimes they felt a commitment to the cause they were fighting for, but they came back to the US alone. They returned to families and a society that didn't necessarily appreciate, and certainly didn't understand, their suffering and experience. Many were unable to resume their former lives. Some became homeless, suffered PTSD, committed suicide or even homicide, had health issues, and never adjusted. Being part of a *whole*, rather than being an *individual*, is a fundamental difference between Mai's culture and that of the US.

We were quiet as we left the Vietnam Wall and walked down the National Mall. Mai loved the statue of Franklin D. Roosevelt. She pushed her wheelchair up to the sculpture of the former president and talked to it.

Well, my friend, here we are, two people in wheelchairs. We have seen the world from a different perspective than most people. I am glad to meet you. I notice your wheelchair is underneath your cloak. Join me for a tour of Washington because we can easily travel in our chairs together.

In Vietnam, we wouldn't be able to travel a block by ourselves without running into an obstacle.

By now there was a group of us—my children, Nick and Maria Mai, my former husband, David, his wife, and two former AFSC staff—gathered in Washington, DC, to visit with Mai. We took her to the Society of Friends Meeting House for Sunday worship. With a walled garden and simple interior, the historic meeting house was an oasis of calm. No ornamentation and plain glass, not stained glass, in the large windows let an almost mythical, protective glow fill the space. Mai knew Quakers sit silently in rows of benches facing each other. Like all of us, she was quiet and alone with her meditations.

It is rare for someone to speak. But a birthright Quaker, David Bailey, who was on the AFSC team in Quảng Ngãi and had come to Washington to meet Mai, stood up. He addressed those gathered and shared that among them was a woman named Mai who had worked at the AFSC Rehabilitation Center in Vietnam, supported by private funds from Quakers like those in the meeting room. When David finished speaking, Mai indicated that she wanted to speak and asked if I would translate what she was about to share. The core of her message was to thank the Society of Friends and AFSC for its work in Vietnam and its mission to treat Vietnamese as people, not as the enemy. Mai said their programs "saved my life and many others." Can silence become even more silent? We dwelled on the significance of Mai's words. Light streaming through the irregular glass of the old windows was a witness to the memories of an awful war.

Later that day, Mai and Thuy watched Nick play ice hockey. They had never seen a hockey game. As we left our seats at the edge of the rink, the players were shedding their uniforms. There was no private dressing room. Mai tapped one of Nick's teammates with her crutch and said in Vietnamese, "Hey, I'd be a good hockey player, don't you think? I already have my padding. Look. My legs are wood!" The player just stared.

Everywhere she went, including the hockey rink, Mai was amazed at her ease of access. I felt the same way when I returned from Vietnam, in 1974. I saw people in wheelchairs holding hands as they rolled down the street in Berkeley, California, and friends in assisted-living apartments had everything within reach. These scenes brought tears to my eyes. The Vietnamese spirit offered optimism to people with disabilities, but the reality of maneuvering in a rural setting could be discouraging. Mai said she once lived in a sister's house, with uneven dirt floors, unsuitable for her prostheses, and spaces too tight for a wheelchair. She scooted around the house, pushing and pulling her body from a bed to a chair.

One night over dinner, I told Mai about an accessibility challenge in my career that built on my experience in Vietnam. "Mai, I know you are impressed with the ease of mobility for Americans with disabilities," I told her, "but advocates for the disabled fought long and hard for a federal law to bring about these changes." While working as director of historic preservation at the US Treasury, I was "loaned" to the US Department of Justice. On July 6, 1990, President George H.W. Bush was scheduled to sign the Americans with Disabilities Act, followed by a ceremony in the magnificent Great Hall of the Department of Justice. But the marble hall wasn't accessible to wheelchairs, and historic restrictions prohibited major alterations to the structure.

My assignment was to oversee the design of ramps and passageways leading from the building exterior to the Great Hall and onto the stage. More than a thousand attended the celebration. I'd never been with people with so many different disabilities. Although it was startling to be introduced to such a wide variety of ailments, injuries, and congenital conditions, I was gratified to see everyone ably getting around and celebrating this landmark law.

I hadn't spoken about this before, and Mai listened as I stumbled to find the Vietnamese words to describe building preservation and federal legislation. She patted my knee. "Jane, I'm glad you learned something in Vietnam—to live in a world with the disabled. Now we Vietnamese should study the American model and make changes in Vietnam. Access might not be perfect in the United States, but you take accessibility for granted. When I am here, I feel as if the world is open to me."

Mai (foreground) posing before White House with Maria Mai, Jane and Mai's daughter Thuy

I took pictures of Mai in front of the White House. She said she felt "liberated." The White House was one of the seats of power directing the war, and I expected her to note "Vietnam won." Instead, she declared, "It's time for Vietnamese and Americans to be friends and look forward."

Something that surprised me was Mai's nervousness about the isolation of my 1850 farmhouse outside of Washington, DC. "How different from Vietnam, where I can see, hear, and talk to all my neighbors," she said. Not only could I not see most of my neighbors, but I didn't even know their names. Traditional life in Vietnam revolves around villages, hamlets, and districts—rings of connection with people linked to the land around ancestral graves. I had moved twenty or more times in my life, from coast to coast, and like many Americans, I strove to acquire a house and space, solitude, peace, and few neighbors. My farmhouse and my cottage on a remote Maine island are cases in point. Mai worried about not having family nearby to help.

New York City was our next destination. Roadways like the New Jersey Turnpike astonished Mai and Thuy, not just because of the vastness of five lanes of traffic but also the paved surfaces—mile after mile. Thuy wasn't carsick. Roads were smooth, and cars were air-conditioned. However, just as I was initially disoriented by the horse carts, cars, motorbikes, and people transporting items in Vietnam, Mai was undergoing her own culture shock.

My friend, Marielena, owned a grand apartment on West End Avenue. I arranged tickets to *The Lion King* for Mai, Thuy, and Sophie, who relished seeing Mai again. The performance didn't require English proficiency to understand the theme. Mai and Thuy were thrilled with the costumes and music. That night, even though Marielena had enough beds, Mai, Thuy, Sophie, and I slept on the hard floor, as if in a Vietnamese bed.

We headed for Vermont to stay at a summer home belonging to Keith Brinton's family. AFSC people joined us from across the country. Keith and his wife, Claudia, flew in from California. Keith's brother, a Quaker conscientious objector during the war, like Keith, lived next door to the old Brinton homestead and helped with logistics. The house wasn't quite big enough to accommodate everyone, so a few brought tents to camp on the property. The aim of the gathering was twofold: to meet with Mai and have a mini AFSC Quảng Ngãi reunion. All of us, except for two spouses, had known Mai in Vietnam.

There was also a surprise guest—our "team baby," Glen, now a grown man. AFSC requested none of us have children during our term of service, and our team nurse and doctor, Bev and Chuck, thought they were following orders. However, a "cyst" turned out to be a pregnancy, and Glen was born. He provided wonderful public relations for us. Until he made an appearance, the Vietnamese thought we were a strange breed—without children. Glen proved we could produce babies too.

Baby Glen was a curiosity wherever we went. Women in the marketplace grabbed him from Bev's hands to get a better look and pass him around. The women were enraptured by this chubby, golden-haired child. They sniffed him, an affectionate way to kiss a child. Once, while sitting in the passenger side of our small Japanese truck, a Vietnamese woman reached in my window and thrust her hand down the front of Glen's diaper. I assumed she didn't think White people spoke Vietnamese, otherwise I would have given her the answer: "Yes, Glen is male."

Thirty-five years later, Baby Glen was a professional plumber and had a family. His father, Chuck, the beloved orthopedic doctor, stayed home to take care of their off-the-grid farm in Nebraska, while his mother, Bev, brought cold chests filled with homegrown food. Bev had also spent hours knitting Mai a shawl in muted colors. Mai wrapped the shawl around herself on the cool New England evenings.

Mai wrapped in a shawl handknit by Beverly Henkel, former AFSC staff nurse

There were twenty of us. Former AFSC staff traveled from California, Idaho, North Carolina, Wisconsin, and elsewhere, demonstrating the esteem they had for Mai. We shared meals and sang antiwar folk and Vietnamese songs. We sat in a circle for Meeting for Worship and to share stories. Earl Martin, the Mennonite who stayed in Quảng Ngãi after the liberation, mesmerized us with poetry.

Too soon, Mai and Thuy's trip came to an end. They had easily and comfortably immersed themselves in the United States, and by now, Mai loved riding in elevators. For me, it was the end of yet another intimate encounter with my dear friend. Though we had no specific plans, we knew we would meet again.

Jane Goes to Vietnam

Not much time passed before Mai invited me back. Her US trip had allowed us to visit as normal friends, sharing experiences and meals. Now she wanted me to spend time at her house with her family. My previous trips all had an agenda—to conduct research for *Last Night I Dreamed of Peace*, to interview NLF women as part of a grant, to take my children to visit Vietnam, and to deliver Agent Orange funding. In December 2018, I visited Mai simply as a tourist and friend.

Two former AFSC staff came with me—Diane Jones and Claudia Krich. Another friend would already be in Vietnam, former US prisoner of war Bob Chenoweth. Mai invited Bob to join us. She was waiting at the Tam Ky airport to take us to her new house.

Before the trip, Claudia insisted on staying in a hotel. She wanted to sleep on a mattress, not a hard wooden bed. I also liked the idea of an air-conditioned hotel room. Though we didn't know about Mai's current living situation, we were familiar with her previous dwellings and couldn't imagine how she would house and feed us. We didn't want her to think her house wasn't up to the standard of hosting, but, after all, we were four. We told Mai it was customary in the US for that many guests to seek their own lodging. Mai absolutely insisted we had to stay with her; we were family.

But Mai had a new living arrangement. After Thuy's father-in-law suffered a debilitating stroke, members of the extended family combined their resources. They were especially helped by Thuy's sister-in-law, Dao, whom Sophie and I met in Hanoi in 2005. Dao's salary with an international agency helped build a handsome two-story house for her father. He was now situated in a bedroom with a Western-style bathroom on the home's first floor. There was a big family room and an alcove for a kitchen.

Thuy, her husband, Long, and their two children had multiple rooms on the second floor of the big white house. Mai lived twenty feet away in a small one-story house with a living room, dining area, bedroom, and bathroom. The entire compound was surrounded by a white wall enclosing a tree, plants, and a driveway with a car. A cook came in during the day to prepare some of the meals, including pureed food Thuy's mother-in-law fed her husband, spoon by spoon. The mother-in-law took sole care of her husband. There were no nurses, health-care workers, or US-style Veterans Administration hospitals for Vietnamese war veterans. Long tended to his father's needs during the night. The family took responsibility for the patriarch.

We were escorted to our rooms on the second floor of the in-law's home and then to Mai's house to watch the cook make *bun sao*, a crepe made of rice flour, turmeric, and coconut milk, cooked until crispy on an outdoor coal brazier. I was invited to try my hand at making one. The filling contained shrimp, shallots, and bean sprouts. The whole thing was wrapped in lettuce and dipped in *nuoc mam*—fermented fish sauce.

Ten of us sat around the large table in Mai's house. We ate in typical communal style, using chopsticks to select pieces of food from artfully arranged dishes. I felt overwhelmed by the changes in Mai's living situation. Here she was, hosting us in a pleasant house during this time of peace.

We presented Mai with gifts. She complimented each one. On previous occasions, in the traditional Vietnamese style, she had put the gifts away without opening them. For six days, we were absorbed into the daily life of a Vietnamese family. We took day trips to scenic places in the mountains and to local beaches. Mai's nephew, a medical student in Hue, joined us. Claudia and I laughed at how he walked, one of us on each arm, down the street to a bean drink shop. In the US, a handsome young man would not be likely to go out for bubble tea—pearls of tapioca floating in the glass—linked arm-in-arm with two "old ladies."

We went to a nearby Buddhist temple and sat in the cool courtyard. Mai said it was important we reflect and share. We'd been through dramatic changes in our lives over the past forty years. We recalled missed opportunities for lifelong relationships while acknowledging how content we were as independent women. We wished for a way to live near each other as sisters.

We talked about our friendship, how we found each other again in 2000 when our children met, and how, in 2005, Mai flew to Hanoi to tell Sophie and me her story. This is a letter from Mai when I was working for Save the Children:

> *July 1, 2002*
>
> *Now we two are lonely women—we're more often sad than happy. But making up for that, we have great freedom, endless freedom; nothing affects our daily existence either, nor over a lifespan. You are busy with much useful work for society. Oh, that you may strive with ardor and wholeheartedness to help children on this planet—luckless children who were born in wartime, children poisoned by Agent Orange. It is such bad luck for them. They are children who are suffering; their whole lives are a film of darkness. If there are any social organizations like yours, with luck, they will save a certain number if done with fairness . . .*
>
> *I was glad to learn that your children are studying hard, and they love their mother. Your family is different from mine where mother, father, children, and grandchildren all live*

> together, support one another, and during illness or sadness can share with each other. I only have Thuy, but when I am sad, happy, or sick, there is Thuy and her husband to take care of me. That is my greatest source of happiness. You, Jane, and I are two friends who have not had true family happiness. The war stole what little happiness I managed to have. As for you, wasn't it simply your personal fate? Isn't it possible that you might take just one more step out in the world—perhaps you might have a friend who could make you happier? If so, I would be very glad.
>
> Even though you and I are two different people with different languages, different customs, and different styles of life and activity, I consider you a very close friend, very true, heart-related sister...
>
> What are you doing today, Jane? Are you tired from work? I bet you are really worn out. Let me share your tiredness, okay? Let me share your loneliness, your sadness if you have any. I frequently get the feeling that you are nearby; your image stays with me as if you'd been here just yesterday...

After writing about Thuy's father and his current life, Mai continued.

> On her wedding day, Thuy and Thuy's father came to be with me. His father and all his older sisters also came to visit us. Our friendship is that of really intimate friends. Because that's our future, which didn't turn out the way we wished.
>
> At this time, though, I am very happy without him. I find it easier this way. Because my health isn't good, I can't work the way all my friends do. This regret adds to the burden I must bear in my life because of the war. War stole my youthful years, stole years of burning passion from me. Those young years are for getting experience and doing what one wants to

do. Now I'm old already, and I cannot go traveling here and there. You and your children should never let war terminate your happiness.

Two months later, I wrote back.

What pleased me about your last letter was your ability to be frank and honest with me, to share your feelings, the exhilarations and hardships. I like the Vietnamese custom of sharing what is in our hearts. Please do not be melancholy knowing how busy I am. I am glad that you tell me these things. I, too, am happy enough alone. We are two invincible women who still have a future. We must write a book about our experiences during the war, and that will give us a noble purpose in the years ahead.

I kept another letter Mai wrote two years later, in 2004.

I wish you would come to Vietnam again, Jane. My age is already fairly advanced—I've had sixty-two years filled with joy, sadness, and misery because the war stole my youth away. The war brought bombs, bullets, hunger, and poverty. I grew up during the twenty-year French war, then the fifteen-year American war, and the result is that I'm left with half a body. But I still live on, thanks to you and friends who helped add much joy to my life.

Since 1975, things have gotten much better. Here I am, sitting in my own homeland. This place no longer has war; it is quiet, peaceful. Life has sprouted its green leaves anew. Life is very free and happy. . . . I really remember all the faces of the Quakers individually, friends separated from me by half the circumference of the globe. I want our children to be friends with each other the way we were friends. Although social

> *class differences keep people from truly understanding each other and respecting each other, it is my hope that people can be equal and move up to a world of peace, with no "stronger" versus "weak" people.*

As the time for my departure from Vietnam neared, Mai finally asked if I was going to write a memoir. She startled me by handing me a letter I had written to her—in Vietnamese—in 2003. In it, I committed to writing about Mai and reaffirmed that promise.

Mai and her family went to the station to wave goodbye as I, my AFSC friends, and Bob took the train back to Hanoi. She gave us gifts: a bag of fresh red pepper flakes and several "stalks" of cinnamon bark. Having only seen cinnamon in curled, four-inch sticks, I hadn't realized it came from large pieces of tree bark. I liked that presents could be food, delivered without fancy packaging.

The train ride gave me time to reflect. Mai described herself as "having half a body," but she took that body to Hanoi and the US, enjoyed the experiences to the fullest, and broke through many barriers. Mai proudly displays her artificial limbs and wheelchair. She came to realize her amputated legs could be sexy, she won the right to give birth to her child, and she blended her daughter into two families, Thuy's father's family and Long's family. Mai faced obstacles, emerging as a wartime hero, admired by friends and neighbors. The biggest newspaper in Vietnam featured her story.

Mai lives in a simple, comfortable house next door to her family. Her grandchildren can easily "pop over" to share a meal or keep Mai current about their school and sports activities. It's a changed world. The American government was once Mai's enemy. Now both her grandchildren have studied in the US and gone on to have professional careers.

The war will never be over for Mai and me. It is deeply etched in our memories, the needless pain and suffering. But it is also at the core of a fifty-year friendship that created a small bridge between two disparate cultures.

EPILOGUE
A World Away from Vietnam

MY GRANDSON WAS born with a rare genetic disorder that has caused him to be deaf/blind, so I moved to Boston to support Maria Mai. It was easy to get caught up in my American life, friends, and family. The idea of a book slipped into the background.

But, when the COVID-19 pandemic forced me to isolate, I went to my cottage on an island in Maine and began writing. The words tumbled out, hour after hour.

I had hidden Vietnam inside me for many years, especially after I divorced and needed to resume a career in the arts. I remember telling a friend, in a moment of frustration, that those years of working in Vietnam were wasted because they didn't enhance a résumé designed to help me reenter my former profession. Plus those years brought me pain. I didn't think anyone in my Washington, DC, work circle could relate to my war experience, so I buried Mai and Vietnam deep in my heart to preserve and protect my feelings. It was not a successful strategy. Those intensely fresh emotions from my first day in Vietnam are always with me.

The Watermark

I picked up a book by author Jacques Leslie, a former war correspondent in Vietnam for the *Los Angeles Times*. Jacques was the journalist I smuggled into the prison ward at Quảng Ngãi Hospital to witness tortured prisoners. Reading *The Mark* a second time, I was struck by his description of those deeply affected by the Vietnam War as having "the mark." His reference was immediately clear: I was one of them. He wrote,

> Having the mark meant being addicted to Vietnam, being used to intrigue and pumping adrenaline and layer after layer of lie, truth, lie, truth, until the two were indistinguishable. People with the mark shared a yearning they suspected Vietnam of being able to satisfy and while they hated the war (for wars are meant to be hated), they loved it even more and hated themselves for loving it. In Vietnam I'd found my universe of darkness and light, the font of all my feelings. So deep was my mark ... that it outlived the war by a decade and a half. At first it felt like a blessing, then a curse, and finally a blessing again: at last, I understood that the mark was my destiny, my path, and that in following the path to its end, I had solved the mystery of my life. Then I looked back at my experiences in Indochina and for the first time saw their harmony.[60]

The watermark left by Vietnam on my soul is like that mark on US currency, visible only when held up to the light. Then those indelible memories of Vietnam shine. My watermark guards my secrets. At certain times it has brought pleasure, sometimes pain, but in the end, I cherish the imprint made by my friend, the "enemy", Mai.

---

60 Jacques Leslie, *The Mark: A War Correspondents Memoir of Vietnam and Cambodia*, New York, Four Walls Eight Windows, 1995, Prologue, p.3.

Mai's contribution to this book evolved through long interview sessions. With Mai's approval, Vietnamese translator Nguyễn thi Trang translated all of Mai's quotations and stories, carefully and cooperatively selected by Mai and Jane, into Vietnamese.

After comments and edits from Mai, these sections were translated back into English. Nguyễn thi Trang donated her fees to *Women Who Code*, an international nonprofit.

ACKNOWLEDGMENTS

TO MAI, WHO created the memories I recorded in this book, you have my forever respect, awe, and love.

Frankie FitzGerald, thank you for reading an early draft. I've long admired your book, *Fire in the Lake*, as one of the most important books written about Vietnam. My memories with you include the time we met in Quang Ngai Vietnam and our reunions on Mount Desert and Great Cranberry Island.

Mary Dempsey, you've been a supporter from the start. I am indebted to you for your valuable edits and proofing skills, as well as for our friendship and biweekly Zoom calls.

Eleanor McCallie Cooper, who worked in tandem with me as we both began our book journeys. We sent each other chapters every Friday and Zoomed to critique on Monday. Eleanor's book, *Dragonfly Dreams*, was published in 2022.

Kim Dang thi Tram, the trip to Duc Pho to the site where your sister was killed was one of the most profound experiences of my life. Thanks to your sister Phuong and Mother Tram for sharing time at the Martyr's Cemetery and your country house. Few visitors to Vietnam have been welcome as genuinely as I.

Earl Martin, your book, *Reaching the Other Side*, has always been an inspiration. Your rich vocabulary, sensitive understanding, and interpretation of Vietnamese people is exceptional. I am grateful you wrote an account of the liberation of Quang Ngai; it is unique and, as far as I know, the only English recording of the monumental, mostly peaceful event.

Sophie, your expertise in Vietnam history was a valuable

contribution to our interviews with revolutionary women. I hope our teamwork in recording their stories will be an important historical contribution.

Le thi Linh Chi and Nguyen Hong Yen, you organized a special, nostalgic return trip to Quang Ngai for me with my children, Maria Mai and Nicholas. Linh Chi, I will be forever grateful for your locating Mai and connecting us.

Nguyen thi Thao: superb translator and friend. Thanks to your mother and sisters for hosting Sophie and me. Riding on the back of your motorbike to get pho in the morning is a favorite memory.

MaryBridget Horvath, who I hired to help me with a slew of computer challenges. You then transitioned to being a cheerleader and friend. It was great to work with you. All the Horvaths contributed—Lesley for keeping me upbeat; Nellie and Philip for your help too!

Jane Fonda and Craig McNamara, I appreciate your contributing blurbs for this book.

It was great fun to be invited to speak to your Vietnam History classes at Dartmouth College, Professor Ed Miller, and witness the interest in Vietnam by a new generation in the American war in Vietnam.

Carol Bundy, for organizing the Tavern Club event focusing on the Vietnam war. Carol, you bring special insights to Vietnam's history. It was a terrific feat for you to read, edit, and comment on an early long draft of the book. I look forward to our July Fourth reunions on Cranberry.

Jock Heron, who listened to me describe my experiences in Vietnam at the Tavern Club in Boston and felt it was important history to share with others.

David Lawrence, a Marine captain who served in Vietnam, joined me in speaking to the members of the Tavern Club, and you were one of the first to say you thought I had a story worth recording. I appreciate your introduction to Pulitzer Prize-winner Tracy Kidder.

Tracy Kidder, thank you for your assistance and our email exchanges.

David Bailey, Jessica and Rob Bailey, and Bob and Kathy Redig, it was wonderful to share the return trip to Vietnam with each of you and to plant Peace Trees at My Lai. Exceptional memories.

Sam Martin, my high school heart throb and dear friend, who carefully proofed the manuscript and honored me on my eightieth birthday. You introduced me to Jerry White, whose book, *Romeo and Tuyet*, is scheduled to be published in 2025 thanks to Kim Dang thi Tram.

Marianna and Annie Houston, longtime friends, you listened to me tell many of the stories that are now part of this book. Your love and support over the many years of our friendship has been critical to my life.

Jacques Leslie, it was special to reconnect with you and revisit your description of the female political prisoners in Vietnam in *The Mark*.

Nhu Miller, within your large circle of international contacts, you found a Vietnamese translator in Germany to ensure that all of Mai's words were accurately recorded and introduced me to Jay Schaefer.

I had no idea you or these archives existed, but thanks to you, Donald Davis, AFSC archivist, and the retention of my fifty-year-old photos and reports, this book has been made richer.

Mercury Computer, a small business with expert and kind service, you kept the three computers I purchased from you running, even when I stepped on one and lost another. And blessings to those unknown coincidences that mysteriously conspired to bring my computer, lost on the way home from Antigua at JLK airport, to be deposited on my porch many weeks later in the middle of the night with no notice.

My brother Tom remained supportive of my book project over the years, and my sister-in-law Barbara identified the forget-me-not flowers in my yard that matched those embroidered on a pillow cover by Mai.

David Barton, we made a great team together and shared a deep love of Vietnam and its people.

It was a once-in-a-lifetime experience to have my children, Maria Mai and Nicholas, join me on my first return trip to Vietnam—to a Vietnam at peace. Your appreciation of Mai, planting of Peace Trees, and absorbing the whole Vietnam experience demonstrated your sensitive spirits. I love you both and am glad we shared that memorable trip together. You saw my Vietnam and the new Vietnam.

Lastly, to my friend Elizabeth, who listened to all the ups and downs of the book progress on our frequent phone calls. Thank you for your faith in me.

DISCUSSION QUESTIONS

1) How much did you know about the Vietnam War before you read this book? What did you learn from this story? Did your views about the war change? What more do you want to know about the war in Vietnam?

2) What was it about this book that drew you to it? If you hesitated, what were your concerns?

3) The background of these women were starkly different—Jane's life of privilege in the US and Mai's peasant upbringing in a rural countryside. Describe a friendship you might have formed with a person totally different from you and how you reached across certain barriers.

4) What more do you want to know about these two women and their lives?

5) Some of the themes explored—torture, war, humanitarian service—are relevant to current events today. Give an example.

6) Most books about wars are written by men. How do you think this book is different because it is written by women about women?

7) On two occasions, the US military suggested that the AFSC/Quaker team should evacuate. What would you have done if you had been one of the Western staff at that time?

8) Overtime, things change, especially in relation to war. Countries are no longer enemies. People grow older and change. When Mai came to visit Jane in the US, how had things changed from the time these two women were in Quang Nai together?

9) What did you learn about war injuries and disabilities from this book? What are your thoughts about current wars and the impact of civilian injuries and death?

10) What was your favorite part of the book?

www.ingramcontent.com/pod-product-compliance
Lightning Source LLC
LaVergne TN
LVHW091542070526
838199LV00002B/167